M000200382

A
STONE
CRIED
OUT

257.6
SHI

154

DEEP RUN EAST
LIBRARY

SHIGEO SHIMADA

A STONE CRIED OUT

THE TRUE STORY OF SIMPLE FAITH IN DIFFICULT DAYS

Judson Press® Valley Forge

To
My Children

Gloria
and
Justin

A STONE CRIED OUT

Copyright © 1986
Judson Press, Valley Forge, PA 19482-0851

All rights reserved. No part of this publication may be reproduced, stored in a retrieval system, or transmitted in any form or by any means, electronic, mechanical, photocopying, recording, or otherwise, without the prior permission of the copyright owner, except for brief quotations included in a review of the book.

Scripture quotations are from the Revised Standard Version of the Bible copyrighted 1946, 1952 © 1971, 1973 by the Division of Christian Education of the National Council of the Churches of Christ in the U.S.A., and used by permission.

Library of Congress Cataloging-in-Publication Data
Shimada, Shigeo, 1906-
    A stone cried out.

1. Shimada, Shigeo, 1906-   2. United Methodist
Church (U.S.)—Clergy—Biography.   3. Methodist Church—
United States—Clergy—Biography.   I. Title.
BX8495.S542A3   1986   287'.6'0924 [B]   86-20152
ISBN 0-8170-1111-0

The name JUDSON PRESS is registered as a trademark in the U.S. Patent Office.
Printed in the U.S.A.

Acknowledgments

This book would never have been written if it were not for Anne King Craig's patience and insistence that I write my story. I am grateful to her for her interest in my life story and for all the valuable advice she gave me.

I am grateful to Mr. Glenn M. Barns for his interest, encouragement, and assistance in the early stages of my project. His review and constructive criticism were significant contributions toward publishing this book.

Contents

1

"This Is America!"

The customs inspector at San Pedro harbor was a huge man, tall and fat. He towered over me. He seemed a giant, almost a Goliath. I knew American professors and missionaries in Japan, but none of them were so tall nor so wide. I was—and still am—five-feet-three-inches tall, which was not small in Japan. In front of the inspector I felt like a dwarf. He was a redwood tree; and I a *bonsai*, a dwarf tree of Japan.

Still, I was calm and smiling. This man was important; he had power over me; he was the last possible obstacle to my entry into America after the fifteen-day journey from Kobe, Japan; but I was sure he would be satisfied with the answers I gave to his questions.

The other seven passengers on the freighter had passed the inspector without any trouble. Two of them were American missionaries returning home; the others were businessmen. I was the only student. I was twenty-nine years old and unmarried. I had plenty of money and a good scholarship at the School of Theology of Southern Methodist University. I had never been in any trouble with the police.

The inspector ordered me to come into his office with him. He examined my suitcases. I remained confident and smiling; I certainly was not a smuggler. I was sure there was nothing in my two battered, old suitcases to cause him distress. I still remember the contents. There were some Western clothes— shirts, underwear, socks, and so forth, all made in Japan—and a brown kimono which I thought I might wear on rare occa-

9

sions. There were my three Bibles: English, Japanese, and Greek. And there were three cans of fish balls and one can of rice cookies. These—with my towel, soap, and other toilet articles—were the entire contents of the suitcases. Nothing to cause me trouble there.

The year was 1935. I remembered the tears of the church members who had come to see me off at Kobe Harbor. They were all crying, and I had been embarrassed because I did not feel the sadness natural to a person leaving his native country. I had tried to pretend to be sad, but my heart had been singing, because I was going to a Christian nation, and to me it was a wonderful thing.

"How much money do you have?" the inspector asked.

I was prepared for that question. I knew, of course, that I would not be admitted to America if I could not show that I was able to support myself. In Japan the members of my church and my personal friends had raised 1,200 yen for me, a huge sum. When I exchanged it for American dollars in the Sumitomo Bank, it became only $300, perhaps not so huge a sum, but still a great deal of money. The ticket on the freighter had cost $100. I had a lot of money, in addition to my scholarship.

Just before leaving Japan one of my professors in the School of Theology had said to me, "Mr. Shimada, you have $200. You are the richest theological student I ever heard of. When I went to America ten years ago to study, I had only ten dollars in my pocket. You are certainly rich and do not need to worry about money at all."

And so I was calm and confident when I answered his question, "Two hundred dollars, right here, right now. Shall I show you, sir?"

I was expecting him to be surprised that a little Japanese student like me had such a huge sum of money. Perhaps I was a little more proud than I should have been. I certainly did not expect to see him frown.

"Is that all?" he asked.

Was that all? The question startled me. I lost my confidence; I felt nervous and knew I was probably pale. Naturally I had expected $200 to be considered a great deal of money, even in America. Surely it was twenty times as much as the ten dollars my professor had told me about. But it did not impress this big man at all.

"Yes, that's all, sir," I said. "But don't you think $200 is enough for a student?"

Now he was surely frowning at me. "No, $200 is a very small amount of money. I'm afraid you know nothing at all about college expenses. I am a college graduate myself, and I lived as cheaply as possible. I still needed $600 a year. How can you expect to study in America with such a small amount of money as $200?"

His words turned my fortune into nothing. They changed me from the richest student to the poorest student in no time. I realized that I was in a mess, and I almost lost control of myself. I was trembling and shaking. Then I remembered my most important asset, the thing that would surely convince him.

"Mr. Inspector," I said, "the School of Theology of Southern Methodist University in Dallas, Texas, promised to give me $300 a year as a scholarship. I have here a letter about it from the school." I handed the letter to him.

He read it carefully. I watched him, almost holding my breath. I was certain the letter would make things all right, but his frown did not relax as much as I hoped it would.

"This is a good scholarship," he said. "Now you have $500 altogether this year. If you cut your personal expenses very closely, you will probably be able to study this year. But how about next year?"

Now the man was even worrying about the problems of next year! No one knows about next year. There is a proverb in Japan that says, "If you talk about anything of the next year, the devil (in hell) will laugh." I was almost tempted to quote that proverb to the inspector to make him see how foolish it was to worry about the financial situation of next year, but I realized he might not consider this a sincere attitude. Besides, it was not a Christian thought or proverb.

I knew I must not say, "I will work and get enough money to cover all necessary expenses." One of my professors had warned me that foreign students were not supposed to have jobs in America. So to say "I will work" would surely be my ticket back to Japan.

I was tempted to say: "I have a friend in America who is rich; he will help me." When I opened my mouth to tell that lie, the words just did not come out. I still had a little conscience.

The very next moment I realized that not telling the lie was not only a matter of conscience but good sense. His other questions would have come very fast. "Who is this rich friend of yours? What is his name and address? What is his telephone number?" My inability to answer those questions certainly would have been my ticket back to Japan.

The inspector was waiting for my answer, but I was at a complete loss. I did not know what to do or say. I really wanted to cry, but that would not have been helpful at all.

I closed my eyes and knelt down before the inspector. It might have looked as though I were praying to him, but of course I was not. Silently, and not ashamed or caring what anyone who might see me would think, I was praying to God.

"God, I came to this spot on the earth. I thought that it was your will that I come to America, but I am stuck here completely. This inspector has been pushing me into a corner. If he sends me back to Japan, I feel I would have to commit the honorable *hara-kiri*. Oh, God, please help me."

This prayer was a cry for help from the heart, and it overlooked my genuine Christian belief that suicide is a sin. In my despair and confusion, I was voicing the traditional thinking of the Japanese since the age of feudalism. When a man "lost face" in a serious matter, the only way of atonement was the honorable suicide, or hara-kiri.

It was a short prayer, and far from ideal because of its reflection of pagan ideology, but it was sincere, and that is all any prayer really has to be. When I rose to my feet, my fear had vanished, and I was calm and not trembling anymore.

When I looked at that tall and fat inspector again—that Goliath—I no longer felt that he was a redwood tree trying to crush a little Japanese bonsai. He was quite an ordinary man. The prayer had changed me and the entire situation. It had made me a big man, in faith if not in size. I recognized the strength of prayer.

"Mr. Inspector," I said, "I thought I was a rich student because I had $200. Now I learn that I am a poor student. I do not at this moment know how to get enough money for next year. But let me tell you what I am thinking now. I was a minister in Japan. I was in charge of a small church in Osaka City for two years. My salary was only fifty yen a month, about fifteen dollars in American money. Yet, it was plenty to support me. Whenever I needed more money to give better service to God and to my people, I prayed to God to help me. He helped me every time, not always in the way I expected but in his own way. Now, I am a stranger here in America. I know nothing about this country. At this very moment I must know one thing. I have to ask you one question, which is very important to me. Would you answer it?"

He was a patient man and not so terrifying after all. "All right," he said, "I will answer the question if I can."

"Thank you." I looked at him seriously. "Is there God in America?"

I was sincere and earnest in asking this question, not because of any doubts within myself but because I felt that I could make him understand only if the words came from his own lips. I was sure his own answer would open the iron curtain which he himself was raising before me. To me it was a matter of life and death. He was surprised by the question.

"Of course we have God in America," he said. "America is a Christian nation, you know."

"Thank you, thank you very much indeed. That God in America is the same God who helped me in Japan. If I need money, I will certainly ask God, and I am sure he will help me."

I had said enough. When I looked at him, the frown was gone.

"Reverend, may I have your passport?"

It was as simple as that. His attitude, his tone of voice, everything was changed. He put his signature—the most important thing in the world to me at that time—on my passport. Without it I could not land in America. It meant more to me than a million dollars. When he handed the passport back, I felt as if a new heaven on earth had appeared before me.

The inspector carried my suitcases for me. He opened the door of his office for me. He said, "Reverend, I hope you enjoy your student life in America. May God bless you."

When I heard his words, my eyes blurred with tears. I had been persecuted in Japan in one situation after another: in my high school, in the army, and even in my own home, all because I was a Christian. But here in America, the very first person I met treated me like a king because I was a Christian minister.

In front of the inspector's office I put down my suitcases and looked around me.

"This is America!" I said.

2

A Tempting Penny in a Shrine

E ntry into the United States was not the real crisis of my life up to that time. Before that had come my conversion to Christianity.

I was not born into a Christian household. I would not want anyone to think I mean that as the slightest criticism of my mother and father. They were earnest, sincere people who certainly did the best they could in every way. They had, however, never been given an opportunity to learn anything about Christianity.

My family was of the Buddhist faith, but they were not deeply religious people. They lived as they were taught and believed as they had been brought up to believe, but religion did not play a strong part in our daily lives.

I myself was antagonistic to the gods. I thought their job was to punish people. I believed that when the gods were short of customers, they set traps and enjoyed punishing poor, unsuspecting sinners. At least, at the time I thought I was antagonistic to the gods. I know now that I was always really searching for a faith in which I could put my heart.

This feeling against the gods began with me on a sunny spring morning when I was about six years old. Two friends and I came across a little shrine of four stone images of gods. I do not remember exactly what this shrine was; I was a very small boy, who had not thought deeply about such things. It must have been one of the many shrines connected with Shintoism, the national religion of Japan.

I do not remember why we went to that shrine, for it was not a place that held any attraction for children. I think we just happened to be passing by and dropped in out of curiosity. We were not interested in any house of the gods; we certainly did not respect those stone images. And most certainly we did not go there to worship.

These stone images did not resemble the other gigantic, grotesque images in the bigger shrines. They were rather cute, and we were not in the least afraid of them. In fact, we felt important in front of them, because we were bigger than they were. One of them had a little red bib around his neck. It looked so funny that we broke into laughter. A god with a bib was unthinkable even to a small boy.

The tallest god was about one-and-one-half feet high; the one who had the red bib was the smallest, about ten inches tall. I thought he was a baby god. We classified them as second-class gods in the society of gods, because their shrine was old and shabby, and the gods themselves were so small.

There was an offering box, made of heavy lumber, in front of them. It was too large for these small gods. I personally thought they were greedy, expecting enough offerings to fill this big box. The box was heavy, so heavy that no thief could carry it away.

Out of curiosity I approached it. It was "M" shaped, and there was a long opening in the center. A coin should slip quickly to the bottom of the box, but to my surprise one penny was resting on the sloping surface and seemed to be smiling at me. What a joy and what a temptation it was! It was one of the greatest temptations in the early days of my life.

"Hey, kids, look what I found," I shouted. "A friendly penny."

They came and looked at it and sighed. We all came from families who were very poor.

"What shall we do? Shall we take it?" I asked.

"Let's take it and buy some cookies and enjoy ourselves," one of my friends said.

I agreed with him 100 percent, but the other fellow said, "Wait a minute. We mustn't take it. It belongs to those stone gods."

I agreed with him too, perhaps not quite 100 percent. These were only second-class gods, and I felt no particular respect for them. Still they were gods, and presumably they had some sort of power.

My two friends quarreled with each other for a while about the penny. Neither would give in. Finally they said to me, "You decide. Whatever you say is all right with us."

That made it a fine situation. I had become the leader of the gang, and it was up to me to make the choice. That wasn't easy, because I was divided between the two sides myself. My conscience whispered in a small, shy voice, "You must not take it." My appetite howled in a roaring, aggressive voice, "Don't hesitate, it's yours; take it and buy anything you like."

My appetite won the argument, of course. I did look carefully at the gods to see if they were going to make any protest, but they did not seem to be angry. I said to them silently, "Thank you, gods. You are nice guys after all. I like you." And I took the penny.

We hurried to a little candy shop near the shrine and bought some cookies. They were cheap but tasted good to us. Still, we did not enjoy them as much as we had expected. We did not feel well, not because of a stomachache but because of a little conscience-ache. Even these very small second-class gods might possibly . . . .

We talked the matter over and decided we would keep this business a great secret and not tell anyone about it until death. We hooked each other's little finger as a token of our sacred pledge, and we finally returned to our homes, pretending to have been perfectly good boys.

However, within a few hours our secret spread all over the neighborhood. The mother of one of my two friends came storming to my mother. "Listen," she said, "your son is no good. He stole the gods' money this morning and bought some cookies, and my son and your son ate them together. I have never heard of such a terrible story in my life. Those stone gods are small in size, but they can be very angry. Do something before they get angry; otherwise, a terrible thing might happen to your son."

My mother was a simple woman. Her face turned pale with

fright. She rushed to me and asked, "Shigeo, did you steal the gods' money?"

Her worried look made me realize that I had made a serious mistake. A quick answer was necessary. I said the first thing to come to my mind.

"Mother, I did not steal the gods' money. You see, I was a very good boy in the shrine, so the gods gave that penny to me as a reward. I just took it and said 'Thank-you' from the bottom of my heart. That's all."

I told myself it was a true story. Anyway, it was at least half true. I was more or less convinced that if those stone gods had wanted to keep that penny, they would have kept it deep down inside the offering box where it belonged. Then it would have been absolutely impossible for me to take it. Since the penny had been on the surface of the box, I almost convinced myself that those tender-faced gods loved a little boy like me and had given the penny to me. At least, it seemed a very good story to me, so I just about believed it myself.

My mother did not accept my excuse. According to her judgment I was 100 percent guilty. Early the next morning while the rest of the family was still asleep, she woke me.

"We are going to the shrine to ask forgiveness," she said.

I was very sleepy, but I knew I had no choice. It took only fifteen minutes to walk to the shrine. The stone gods seemed to be sleepy too. My mother knelt down humbly, and I reluctantly knelt down beside her. She seemed to be praying, but I did not know how to pray nor what to do.

"Mother, what shall I do here?" I asked.

"Well," she said, "you just say, 'Honorable gods, I am very sorry. I will never steal again as long as I live. So please forgive me.'"

It should not have been difficult for me to say those few simple words, but somehow I felt silly. After all, they were dumb stone dolls, weren't they? I knew they were unable to hear; it was certainly ridiculous for me to speak to them. I hesitated to repeat the words.

Mother watched me impatiently and finally became angry. "Why don't you ask for forgiveness?"

"Mother, do you really think they can hear us?"

She thought for a long time before answering. "Well," she said, "everybody else prays to these gods, so I imagine that somehow they can hear us."

"But how? They have feet but they can't walk; they have mouths but they can't speak; they have hands but they can't use them. How can they hear us?"

My mother hesitated again before she spoke. "We came here to ask forgiveness, so let's just do that. It's not our concern whether they can hear us or not."

I told myself that Mother was right. We had come to ask forgiveness; it didn't matter whether they could hear me or not. It was a job to get finished. I spoke aloud, repeating the words Mother had given me and adding some of my own: "From now on, please keep all the pennies deep down in the offering box so that a good little boy like me can't take them and get in trouble. Understand?" I was half serious and half angry and felt perfectly silly.

Then my mother took out her little purse from the sleeve of her kimono and picked out a large coin worth two cents. A two-cent coin was common in my childhood days in Japan. I knew she was going to offer it to the stone gods.

"Mother, I took only one penny," I said. "Just pay back one penny." I thought to myself, *Boy, I sure wish she would give that extra penny to me.*

"Well," she said, "I think gods like to receive some interest on their money, so I am giving them 100 percent interest. I hope they appreciate it and forgive you 100 percent in return."

It sounded like a wonderful idea to me. If I had been a stone god, I would have been glad to get an extra penny.

On the way home we were happy since we were quite sure that I was perfectly forgiven. I was pleased to get out of the scrape so easily. We sang merrily as our *geta* (wooden clogs) clattered on the unpaved but hard road.

I had hoped this incident was all behind me, but I was not so lucky. That evening my left arm became painful, and I could not sleep well. The next morning the palm of my left hand had turned red. It looked terrible; I knew something was very wrong. But I had to hide it from my mother for a while because I had a very important job to do that morning. I wanted to find out who had broken our sacred pledge in the shrine, and I wanted to give the guilty one a hard blow in the name of justice.

I went to the house of one of my two friends and called out his name: "Masao!"

His mother came out instead. She was the one who had told my mother about the stolen penny. She gave me a cold glance; then she saw the red palm of my left hand. She seemed gratified, and shouted at me in a shrieking, accusing voice, "I knew it! I knew it would happen to you! Now those stone gods are punishing you. Look at your left hand. It's getting rotten like leprosy. You will have to cut off your arm from the shoulder; otherwise you will die soon."

These words were a big blow to a six-year-old boy. I was very frightened. The woman seemed to take delight in my terror.

"I bet you stole that penny with your left hand," she said.

I remembered that I had used my right hand. I knew I always used my right hand in picking up anything. "No, no, I took the penny with my right hand."

That woman realized that I was a right-handed boy, but it made no difference to her. "Well," she said, "sometimes even gods make a slight mistake when they are in haste, but you have no right to make any complaint. You must accept their punishment with thanksgiving."

I was so terrified that I could not stay there any longer. I ran away from her and came home crying. I seldom cried when I was a child so my mother knew something was very wrong. She stopped her housework and came rushing out.

"What happened this time?" she asked.

"Mother, look at my hand. Those bad stone gods are punishing me. It's getting rotten. What shall I do?"

She looked at my hand and was shocked, not because it looked so terrible but because she actually believed the gods were punishing me.

Early the next morning my mother took me again to the shrine to ask forgiveness. This time I really hated to see those idols. But my mother, humbly kneeling down, prayed in a sincere manner and offered two cents again. I stood there, angrily looking at the gods. Why couldn't they be satisfied with the first extra penny? I began to believe they were trying to get more money from my mother by utilizing her son's guilt. Poor Mother! She promised to come to the shrine with me every morning for two weeks, bringing two pennies every time, and she asked forgiveness in return.

Except for one heavy, rainy day she and I actually went to the shrine every morning during the following two weeks and paid two cents every time. The incident started with only one penny, but it certainly turned out to be an expensive affair. I saw why that shrine had a large offering box.

As far as my hand was concerned, it was a little infection that was healed with some simple ointment within ten days. I wanted to quit going to the shrine, but my mother ordered me to go with her until her promise was fulfilled. On the very last day she thanked the gods for their mercy upon her son. She believed my hand was healed because of the mercy of those stone idols.

On the last day I was extremely angry at them. I said to them in my heart, *You are no good. You are a bunch of bad stone people. I hate you all. When I grow up, I'll kill all of you and destroy all the shrines in Japan, so that you bad guys won't get any money from anybody by using tricks.*

And so from the age of six I had a bad impression of the gods. To me they were all the same; they were treacherous and wicked. They set traps, and if any child was tempted and took something from them, they expected to get it back with large interest. That was their job. They were bad guys.

Such was my conception of gods at that time, and that gloomy idea remained in my heart for ten years. This outlook naturally made me a gloomy, sullen sort of boy.

3
Persimmon Thieves

T he two comrades who helped me steal the penny from the shrine and I were known in the neighborhood as a little gang. I was six years old, and my two friends were five; so naturally I was the leader. Our gang was infamous for its mischievous activities. Fall was a busy season because the persimmon tree in the neighborhood had abundant fruit. Naturally it was our major target.

One day the three of us met in our headquarters (an abandoned hut) and made a perfect plan. We decided to attack the target that day. My two friends were the guards, and I was to perform the major job. I climbed over the tall fence and entered the backyard of the house. It was easy for me to climb over that tall fence because I was a human monkey when it came to climbing. The high persimmon tree in the yard also was easy for me to climb. Within no time I was at the top of the tree. There I chose four ripe, attractive fruits. Why four? One for each guard and two for me.

Congratulating myself for the job well done, as usual, I climbed down, but to my shock and dismay the lady of the house stood there waiting for me to come down.

"Shigeo again?" she said. She knew my name. In fact, all my neighbors knew my name. She grasped my hand strongly and ordered me to sit down at the foot of the tree. I knew I had to obey her because I was now a defenseless prisoner.

My comrades ran away, crying. As I sat down and looked at the lady, she took the fruits from my kimono pocket.

"Wait here," she said. "Don't try to escape. I will bring a rope and tie you up to the tree." She gave me one scolding look and disappeared into the house.

It was a good chance for me to escape, but somehow I did not feel like running away. One reason was that it was of no use because she knew me well, and I knew her well, too. In fact, she was my favorite lady in my neighborhood, for she was always smiling. However, she was not smiling this time. *It was rather fun*, I thought, *to be her prisoner*. I had another reason: Once I put those four fruits in my pocket, they belonged to me. They were mine, and she had no right to take them away from me. She simply had to give them back to me. That was my logical thinking at that time.

The lady came out with a rope and tied me to the tree. "Don't try to run away. You have to be punished. When I think you are punished enough, I will come back and let you go home." With these words she went inside the house again.

It was not a difficult thing for me to loosen the rope and run away, but I decided to remain tied to the tree until she came back. Maybe she would give me back my fruits. I patiently waited and waited and waited, but there was no sight of her. My patience came to an end, but I was not about to cry like my two comrades. I started to sing a patriotic song that was very popular at that time among all the Japanese, young and old.

This song had ten stanzas altogether, and I had learned them all simply because the song told a story about two brave soldiers who were sent to Manchuria with their comrades in the regiment to fight the war. One soldier was severely wounded during the battle. When the other tried to help him, the wounded soldier said, "Don't care for me. Go forward with the others and fight for our country." Thus the brave soldier died in the battlefield.

The story had a sad ending, but it was a heroic song. I was singing as loudly as I could. When I came to the last stanza, the lady came out, smiling and said to me, "You are good in singing. I like the way you sing, so I will give you a reward."

Just as I had reasoned, she gave me back those four fruits. *See, I told you*, I said to myself confidently.

When I was released and came out of the yard, my two

friends appeared from nowhere. "Is everything all right?" they asked. "You don't need to go to jail, do you?"

"Oh no. I'm all right now." I replied.

When I gave each one a persimmon fruit, they were surprised. "Did you steal again after you were caught?" one of them asked.

"Oh no. These fruits are a reward from the lady."

They were utterly confused. They saw me get caught and get tied to the tree. Then they ran away. They simply could not figure out the relationship between stealing and reward, and they were hesitant about eating the reward. When I explained that the fruits were not a reward for stealing but a reward for my singing, they understood and enjoyed the fruits.

The tree-ripened persimmon fruits were simply delicious. *They were worth all the trouble they got us into*, we thought. But I said to my comrades, "From now on we better not steal any fruits anywhere."

They both agreed with me, and we actually stopped stealing completely. After all, the lady with the nice smile taught us a great lesson. I still remember her smiling face.

4

The Eclipse in
My Life

My parents were simple people, who lived without questioning the traditional way. Theirs was a good marriage; they were good people who loved each other. I think they were fortunate in this because theirs was an arranged marriage. They met for the first time on their wedding day—they had not even seen a picture of each other before the ceremony.

The philosophy of the arranged marriage is that "love comes after marriage." It worked out that way for my parents, but they were lucky. I could never consider that type of marriage for myself.

I once asked my father, "Suppose on the wedding day you discover that your bride is a very ugly woman; what can you do? Do you have the right to refuse her on your wedding day?"

My father obviously thought this a strange question. "I don't know," he said. "I never thought about it."

In their case the problem did not arise. My mother was a beautiful woman. She was tiny and slender, with lovely black hair and brown eyes. My father was a handsome man. Much more important, of course, were the character traits that brought them so close and made them mean so much to each other.

If they were fortunate in their love for each other, there were other ways in which fortune did not smile. We were very poor. This was perhaps more difficult for them because they both had been born in different circumstances. My mother was the daughter of a well-to-do businessman in a neighboring town.

My father was the son of a middle-class businessman in Toyama, in the northwest part of Japan. His father once had a prosperous industry, but after the Sino-Japanese War (1904–1905) he lost his business.

My parents moved to Kanazawa, a larger city, and my father became a public school teacher. This was a decent and respectable job, really ideal for his tastes and talents, but the salary was very small. In my father's day teachers' salaries in Japan were very low, and his situation was complicated by the fact that he did not become a teacher until he was over thirty years old. He had to start with a beginner's salary—the same salary paid a single man or woman just out of school. Since he already had a wife and three children to support, things were very difficult for him.

And so my parents had a difficult financial struggle. My mother had to work, making fishing nets with a simple machine and selling them to a store. She worked hard, she was careful with expenditures, but poverty was still a regular visitor in our home.

I was the first son. My sister was already three years old when I was born, and my two younger brothers followed me three years apart. It seemed a miracle that a tiny woman like my mother could give birth to four healthy children. Supporting us was difficult, but I know she did not regret it. She was proud of us. To her we were the greatest treasures in the world. I am sure my father felt the same way.

Still, it was painful to her when she could not give us the things other children had, could not do for us things she felt should be done. I will never forget my very first arithmetic test in the first grade.

"Tomorrow you will have an arithmetic test," the teacher said, "so bring a sheet of paper of regular size."

That evening I asked my mother for a half-penny to buy five sheets of paper. I told her that I would use one for the test and use the rest for the next times.

"I'm sorry, Shigeo, but I can't spare a half-penny today. I have some paper here I can give you."

It was a sheet of paper, all right, but it was full of wrinkles and obviously secondhand. I couldn't face the thought of taking it to class. I was, of course, still a very small boy.

"I don't want to take this old wrinkled paper; the others will laugh at me. Please give me a new one. I promise I will bring home a good mark on it."

But unhappy as this made her feel, she simply did not have half a penny that day. She pressed the paper with her hand, trying to smooth out the wrinkles. It helped some, but not much. I took that paper to school, where everybody except me had a new sheet of paper. I tried to put it out of my mind.

The next day I discovered that I was the only one who had a perfect mark on the test. I was so happy that I did not care whether my paper was old and wrinkled or new and shiny. It did not matter at all.

That evening when I showed the old, wrinkled paper with the perfect mark to my mother, she surprised me by starting to cry. "Please forgive me, Shigeo. I'm very sorry that I could not give you a new sheet of paper."

"Mother, please don't feel bad about it," I said. "It's not the paper that's important, but the mark itself, isn't it?"

I like to think that the knowledge of a more mature set of values I had gained was a comfort to her. I know that she seemed pleased, and that she kept that paper for a long time.

Mature values or not, I was worrying about paper for my next test even while I was comforting my mother. Would she be able to buy it for me? It was still important to me.

A few days later the son of a wealthy man came to school with a pile of new papers about an inch thick. The teacher was not there yet, so he stood up on the teacher's desk and proudly showed the class the paper.

"Get in the back of the room," he said, "and I'll toss this paper up in the air. When it scatters you can pick it up. It's for keeps. And the one who gets the most will get a treat to omanju" (Japanese cake with bean paste filling).

That paper was a great temptation to me. I was eager to get it, almost hungry for it. I knew that if he tossed a thick pile of paper into the air, it would not scatter but would fall straight down. I stood near the desk, where I thought the paper would fall and refused his advice to go to the back of the room.

He tossed the paper, and, just as I expected, it dropped right before my eyes. I picked up the whole pile.

The rich boy didn't like that at all, as he had wanted to show off by having the whole class scramble for the papers. This way it was no fun for him.

"Give me back my papers," he said.

I refused to do that, reminding him that they were "for keeps." I held him to the omanju, too, although he tried to back out. When I insisted, he gave in because he knew that if it came to a fist fight I would win.

On the way home from school he bought two omanju, one for each of us. I still remember how good that cake tasted. I rarely got such a treat at home, and this time I did not have a guilty conscience about stealing the penny.

The incident of the test led to my learning something else as well; this time, about girls. Scholarships are prized in Japan, even among the younger children. My perfect score on the test made me a hero among my classmates. It made Yuriko notice me.

Yuriko was really a sort of princess in that class. She always wore the prettiest kimono. She was perhaps a little chubby, but that didn't matter because she had beautiful eyes. We boys all admired Yuriko and tried hard to get her attention. She didn't seem especially interested in any of us, and definitely paid no attention to me; I was always poorly dressed.

After that test—which, fortunately or unfortunately, depending on the point of view, she had flunked—I became somebody to her. As soon as she discovered that I scored the highest mark, she began to pay plenty of attention to me. She begged me to help her whenever we had an arithmetic test, and I promised to do so.

A few weeks later we had another test; this time it was much easier. There were ten problems altogether, and I finished them in no time. Yuriko, who could not seem to get the answer to any of them, looked at me with pleading eyes. As she sat across the aisle from me, it was easy for me to help her.

The answer to the first problem was "six." While the teacher was not looking, I showed her six fingers, using both hands. Yuriko understood my sign and wrote down an answer; I could tell that it was right by the movement of her pencil. The second answer was "eight." I showed her my eight fingers, and she wrote that down too. The third answer was "ten." I opened both hands, spreading out all my fingers. That beautiful girl only looked confused; she began to count my fingers one by one, taking a long time. I was disgusted. I thought she was never going to finish because she had to keep starting over whenever the teacher turned our way and I had to put my hands down. It was a good thing none of the answers were higher than ten, or I would have had a difficult time figuring out signs she could understand. Eventually she got all the answers down.

The next day I found another perfect mark on my paper. Yuriko, however, had flunked again! I couldn't believe it until I examined her paper. Then I really was utterly disgusted. She had put the answer I gave her to the first problem under the second question, and so on for all of them throughout the whole test, with the last answer under the first question. It was hard for me to see how anyone could do a thing like that.

The worst of it was, she didn't seem a bit upset. She just said, "I don't care whether it's a good mark or a poor one. It doesn't matter at all."

That completely finished my interest in Yuriko, though she was still the prettiest girl in class. I guess it was fortunate for me to have such a graphic illustration of "beautiful but dumb" in early boyhood. I have always kept that in mind when I see a beautiful woman. I think back to the first grade and ask myself: "Could she be dumb, too?"

That is another objection to an arranged marriage, one that could not be overcome by the exchange of pictures.

There came a time when I learned that poverty and all the troubles which go with it are not really troubles at all because I found out what tragedy is. I lost my mother.

Mother was a hard worker. She worked all day long and often at night. I frequently watched her for a long time making fishing nets, not because it was fun to watch, but because I wanted to be with her.

One day she became very ill. The doctor said it was an advanced stage of tuberculosis. We did not tell her, but she knew it was a hopeless case. She was very sad, thinking how her four children would suffer after her death. I was sad too and did not know how to comfort her. I wanted to be comforted myself and be strengthened by somebody, but all in my house were in deep sorrow. Smiles were no longer seen among us. There was no laughter. Even a bright sunny day was dark and gloomy to our family. And finally, the darkest day came.

Mother called me to her bedside and said "Shigeo, you are my first son. Your responsibility will be heavier after my death. Please, take good care of your two younger brothers."

"I will, Mother." I could think of nothing else to add though I desperately wanted to comfort her.

She smiled at me and I tried to smile back. It was more than I could manage. I simply could not do it.

She died that night. My father, my sister, and I were with her when she passed away. My sister cried aloud, but my father held my hand and said, "Don't cry, my son. Remember, you are a boy."

I was in fact just eleven years old. Still, I knew that a boy must not show tears to others even in times of deepest sorrow. I went to the attic alone where I wept and wept. Then I came back and pretended that nothing had happened in the attic.

My youngest brother, Takeo, only five years old at the time, was the most grief-stricken of all of us. One evening he was weeping beside me.

"What's the matter?" I asked.

"I want Mommy. I want to see her again."

I did not know how to comfort him. At that moment I saw shining stars in the sky. One of them was especially beautiful.

"Takeo," I said, "look at that shining, twinkling star. That is our mother. You see, our mother went up to heaven and turned into that beautiful star. So whenever you want to see our mother, look at that star and talk to her."

It was all I could think of to tell him, and he seemed comforted by my words. Whenever he became sad, he looked up at that star and talked to his mother.

There were many changes in our home after that. My sister had to quit junior high school and start to work. She was sad about leaving school, but she bravely adjusted herself to the situation.

At the time of my mother's death my father was thirty-six years old. His friends advised him to marry again, but he did not do so for ten years. He did not speak of a reason, but I knew. For one reason, he could not forget his sweet and faithful wife; he wanted to keep the memory of her in his heart. For another, he was afraid that his four children might not be happy if he remarried. To him his children were treasures, and he wanted to keep us all in his arms. Thus for our sake, and for the memory of our mother, he stayed a widower for ten long years.

He was a quiet man who did not talk much, but he was a good father. He cooked for us and washed our clothes. As his salary was small, he had to have an extra job. He made candy boxes and sold them to stores, earning a small but vital amount of money in this way. In the daytime he was a public school teacher; at night he was a laborer. He never complained, because he had hope for his four children.

Whenever I saw him working hard for us, I said to myself, *I will always be a good son to this good father, and someday I will make him the happiest father in the whole world.*

Instead it was my destiny, not because of ill-will but because of the call of an even higher duty, to bring him years of anguish that almost broke his heart.

5

The Fish Is Hooked

I do not know how my sister happened to start going to the Methodist church. One day, when I was fifteen years old, she proudly announced that she had been baptized and had become a Christian. I was shocked and horrified.

At that time in Japan it was not the official policy of the government to discourage Christianity, but sentiment against the Christians was very strong. This was particularly true in my native town of Kanazawa, which was the center or headquarters of one of the largest sects of Buddhism (Western Hongwanji sect) in Japan. It was said that more than one-third of the population of this city of 150,000 was engaged directly or indirectly in business related to Buddhism.

About the year 1900 American and Canadian missionaries began active services in Kanazawa. They built orphanages, girls' schools, and churches.

Monks, priests and leaders of Buddhism became uncomfortable. They started the anti-Christian movement in my native town. They encouraged the city people to be against Christianity. They asked the grade school teachers to teach their pupils that Christianity was a wicked religion. My fifth grade teacher told us that Christianity was evil and that any Japanese who followed it was a traitor to the Emperor. I believed this, and I hated Christianity. Many simple people in Kanazawa came to believe that America was trying to conquer Japan, using Christianity as a tool, and that all American missionaries were spies sent by the American government.

The sum of my beliefs on Christianity came to something like this. Christ, the founder of Christianity, was a very evil man; he was so wicked that he was finally sentenced to death by the authorities and was killed on the cross. This fact itself proved how evil he was. Yet many Americans and Europeans were still believing in him as the Savior. They were certainly foolish people, but we Japanese were not so foolish. All this I had been taught; all this I believed. I was naturally shocked when my sister became a convert to this wicked religion.

I advised her to give up Christianity. I argued with her. She steadfastly refused. Finally I said to myself, *Well, it's none of my business. She likes Christianity and became a Christian. That's all right for her. For myself, I hate this religion, so I will never become a Christian.*

One small, inconsistent thing bothered me. I could not help noticing that after my sister's conversion she became a new person. She was more cheerful, kind, and loving than before. It was hard to understand.

A year later, when I was sixteen years old, she approached me just as I had been expecting her to do.

"My brother," she said, "I think it would be wonderful if you and I went to church and worshiped God together. Don't you think so?"

"No, no," I said, "I don't want to go to a church. I don't like God, I hate him. God and I have been enemies since I accepted a penny from his offering box. I hate temples, I hate shrines, I hate churches. I hate any place where gods stay or hide. Please don't ever ask me again to go to church; it makes me sick."

She was deeply disappointed, but did not give up hope. I can understand now how much this meant to her, how very badly she wanted her brother to share the joyful experience that had come to her. A few weeks later she approached me in a different way.

"My brother," she said, "I know you do not like Christianity, but I think you like American food. You do, don't you?"

Of course I liked American food. I was sixteen years old, with a terrific appetite. I liked everything edible except garlic.

"Yes," I said, "I like any American dish. Are you going to treat me to an American dinner?"

"Yes, I will treat you today. Since this is Sunday, I have to go to church now. I want you to come to meet me in front of the church in about an hour, say at eleven o'clock. I am sure the service will be over by that time. I will take you to a fine American restaurant and buy you a good dinner. Does that sound pleasant?"

My common sense told me there had to be something fishy about all this, but my appetite dictated the answer without any hesitation. What did I have to lose?

"Sure, sure," I said. "I will be there waiting for you in front of the church. You can count on me."

It was a sunny spring day. I went to the church a little before eleven and waited in front for her. I was expecting to see people come out of the building, but instead they were going in. Things were beginning to look more fishy all the time. Still, I was hungry. While my appetite and my common sense were arguing, two husky men came out of the church and stood on either side of me.

"Are you Mr. Shimada?" one of them asked.

"Yes, I am."

"Please come into the church with us."

"Oh, no thank you. I'm just waiting for my sister."

My refusal was polite but firm, but neither the politeness nor the firmness did me any good. They ignored my answer entirely. Each one took me by one of my arms (they were much larger than I) and marched me inside the church. I really had no say in the matter at all. They led me through the church and sat me down in a front seat, while they sat beside me, still holding my arms. I could not escape; I had been kidnapped.

Then the morning service began. I realized that it was all my sister's scheme, but it was too late. There was something fishy, all right, and I was the fish. A hooked fish. Angry at my sister, I turned around to find her in the congregation. It was not difficult because there were only about thirty people present. I wanted to show her how I felt, but there was nothing to do at the moment except give her a dirty look. When I did that she ignored me.

Well, there is no use trying to run away now, I told myself. *I might as well relax and kill an hour. This is just the high price I have to pay for an American dinner.*

I was quiet during the service. When the people stood up, I stood with them. When they sat down, I sat down too. But when they sang the hymns, I was silent. I was only thinking of that magnificent dinner. When the minister began his sermon, I tried to sleep, but I was not in the habit of sleeping in the morning. There was nothing to do but listen to the sermon. The minister's topic was "Jesus Christ on the Cross."

I thought I knew what he was going to say. He would say that Jesus Christ was a good, righteous man killed on the cross by a group of wicked men. All the evil men like them and like me should be punished and sent to hell. I was looking for that kind of threatening sermon.

"Sinners like you and me should go to the cross because of our sins," the minister told us. When he said "like you and me," his finger seemed to be pointing straight at me. He was following the expected pattern.

But the following words surprised and shocked me. "God sent his only begotten Son to the cross instead and let him die in our place. Thus God opened the way of salvation for us all. God chose this paradoxical way because he loved us sinners so much."

The minister went on to elaborate this principal point of his message. I was startled; it was as though lightning struck the core of my life.

I do not know that I can adequately explain the process of such a sudden awakening of the soul. Men are converted in many ways. Some by a gradual evolution, a learning and a strengthening. Some, like myself, in a sudden, blinding flash of light and knowledge. I only know that my soul *was* awakened, and that this message changed my whole life.

I will never cease to be grateful to my sister and the part she played, although I would not want to condone her unorthodox methods or encourage anyone else to use them. I would never recommend any person to use a wrong method for a good end. In most cases it would be more apt to do harm than good.

As far as my sister was concerned, however, we must remember that this was a special situation. She knew me better than anyone else in the world knew me. She knew my stubbornness, my bitterness. She probably even knew the ache for truth and knowledge which lay behind my surly manners. She loved me and did what she did for my sake. It worked out just as she hoped and prayed.

After that spiritual awakening I felt as if a new unknown world were opened wide before me. I recalled an experience from my boyhood days, when I was eight years old and saw the Japan Sea for the first time.

I had learned to swim in a river when I was seven years old. One day I swam across the river, about a hundred and fifty feet. I was proud of my achievement, and often said: "I can swim across the river." "Across the river" was a big expression to a little boy like me.

On the day I mention my father said to me, "My son, I have heard that you swim well. Today I will take you to the sea to swim."

I was excited and thrilled. "Father, I will show you what a good swimmer I am. I will swim across the sea."

"Well, I know how well you can swim in a river," my father said with a smile, "but you cannot swim across the sea."

"Why not?"

"Simply because," he answered, "there is no other side to reach. That's why."

I could not understand what he meant. It was unthinkable that a swimming place called the "sea" had no opposite side.

We walked to the Japan Sea, about five miles from our home. On the way I imagined an enormous river, but whenever I thought of this great, big river called the sea not having any other side, I was lost. It was beyond my understanding.

When we came to a sandy hill, my father said, "My son, it won't be long now."

I was extremely excited and ran up to the top of the hill, and there it was, a great, big river which had no other side! I was overwhelmed and stood there in awe because the sea was so big and so beautiful.

"Oh!" That was all I could say. What a great river this was. There was truly no opposite side. I knew I could not swim across this sea. It was an entirely new world and a new discovery to me.

Now, when I heard the sermon "Jesus Christ on the Cross" that Sunday, I felt as if a great, new world like the Japan Sea appeared before me. I came to realize that there was a strange, glorious world which I had never thought of and about which I had never been taught; yet it had been there all the time.

When my mother passed away, I certainly needed to be comforted by the love of God, but to me God was nothing but a merciless judge of hell. Instead of coming to God, I was trying to run away from him when I needed his love most.

However, here in the church, the minister said, "God so loved you sinners that he sent his only son Jesus Christ to the cross and let him die there, taking your place." What a great teaching it was. What a wonderful salvation it was. I had been seeking such a love, such a salvation for a long time in my heart. Now I had found it. I knew this was the life; this was the truth; this was the hope. I felt I had to learn much more about it. I felt as though I were a new creature, a new being in a new world, even though I was the same old self in the same old world.

When the morning service was over, my sister came to me and asked, "How do you like Christianity?"

My answer was from the heart. "It is wonderful," I said.

My sister was very happy with my reply. It was the reaction she had been hoping and praying for, but she must have had some doubts about starting things off with a method like that.

My spiritual experience, deep and genuine though it was, had not entirely destroyed the hearty appetite which had gotten me there in the first place. As soon as possible I turned the conversation to the subject of American food. My sister hesitated before answering, but finally she spoke.

"Well, my brother, I really wanted to treat you to rice and curry (she considered this the best American food), but I find that it is much more expensive than I can afford just now. In fact, I do not have any money at all this morning, but someday in the near future I will surely treat you. Please wait until then."

I could not feel angry with her, or even deeply disappointed. Something so much more important had just happened to me. I had missed the expected American dinner, but the spiritual nourishment I had received more than made up for it.

It more than makes up for anything.

6

Shower of Brutal Fists

My life changed in many ways that eventful Sunday. Even as we walked home, my sister taught me how to sing hymns and doxologies. I learned some of them in no time. I had always liked to sing secular songs and thought I was a pretty good singer. After I became a Christian, I turned to hymns and gospel songs. I also enjoyed attending the morning services and evening meetings on Sundays and the prayer circles on Wednesday evenings. Instead of reading detective stories and stories of military leaders I turned to Bible stories.

A year later, at the age of seventeen, I was baptized and became a member of the church.

One day I had a chance to offer a prayer for the first time in a prayer meeting. There were only eight or ten people present. Because I was full of gratitude and thanksgiving, my heart was guided to prayer.

> Our heavenly Father, I thank you for your love. You have loved me so much that you have taken away my mother while I was still a little boy. At that time I did not know the meaning of my mother's death. Now I have discovered that her death has been a highway which led me to Christ. Make me your servant, worthy of your great love.

That prayer came spontaneously from my heart. After the meeting the minister asked me whether my sister had taught me the prayer.

"No," I said, "it was my own. Is anything wrong in my prayer?"

"Oh, no, no," he answered, "it was beautiful. It seemed too beautiful for a young boy like you, so I thought your sister might have taught it to you."

(About ten years later, at the time I was ordained, I met this minister again. He told me that when he heard me offer my first prayer, he believed I would become a minister someday.)

But that was in the future. At the time of which I write, all of the changes brought into my life by Christianity were not so pleasant nor so easy to bear.

I was the only Christian in my class in high school. One day a special junior class meeting was announced to be held after school. We did not know the reason for such a meeting, but after school was over we juniors gathered in the auditorium. There were about 150 students present. When the last person entered the auditorium, all the doors were locked so that no one could go out and no one could get in. When I saw this, I felt a chilling premonition.

Then eight or nine students formed a semicircle in front of all the others. This particular group was known as the gangsters of the class. One of them called my name aloud and ordered me to come forward. Now I knew something would happen to me. I could not run away because all the doors were locked. I went forward. They ordered me to sit down in front of their semicircle. One of them pulled a piece of paper from his pocket and read:

> Shimada became a Christian. We all know that Christianity is an American religion and an evil religion. There is a missionary in his church. He is a spy sent from the American government. We all know that, and Shimada knows it too. Yet he is helping that spy. We often see Shimada walking with that American spy and talking to him. Shimada is a traitor to our nation and a rebellious person to our ancestors. Therefore we are going to punish him in the name of justice and patriotism.

The minute he finished reading, they started pounding my head and striking my body with their fists. I was enraged. I felt my blood boiling inside. I shouted with a raging, uproarious voice, unfamiliar even to me. I stood up to fight against them, strangely eager for the joy of battle. The tough students were surprised by my shouts and stepped back. I was in a fighting rage, ready to jump at them. I really wanted to kill one of them. At that moment I heard a small, strong voice in my heart.

Don't fight back; receive their fists calmly. Remember Jesus Christ died for you. This is a good chance for you to think of Jesus Christ on the cross. Don't fight back but turn your other cheek to them.

When I heard that voice in my heart, anger disappeared and was replaced by calmness. I sat down again. They thought that I was a coward after all and that I lacked the courage to fight back. They gathered around me and started to strike me again, all of them shouting. This time I was not angry; I was not thinking of their brutal fists but was meditating on Christ who was crucified for me.

I found that it is easy for any angry man to fight back, but it is difficult to turn the other cheek; only a Christian who is strengthened by the spirit of Jesus Christ can do it. When they finished punishing me, they ordered the other students to go home. They themselves went home, too.

I was left alone in the auditorium. Not a sound could be heard. I stood up and looked around. When I realized there was no one there, the tears ran down my face. They were not resentful tears; they were tears of victory.

I realized that this was only the first trial. There would be a second, and a third, and many more trials in my life. I would try to be ready for the next one.

My faith actually became stronger through this experience. The next day I hesitated to go to school because I felt that all the other students might laugh at me, thinking me a coward. But I told myself that did not matter. I would think only of Jesus Christ. His kingdom was not weakened by this trivial incident in a small high school.

I went to school as if nothing had happened to me the day before, expecting the reaction of the other students to be cold. To my surprise all except the gangsters welcomed me heartily.

"Why are you so nice to me this morning?" I asked some of them. "I had expected a cold reception from you because I did not fight back. Instead, you welcome me as a friend. Why is this?"

They answered, "We certainly expected and wanted you to fight back, and when you stood up angrily, ready to fight, we whispered to one another, 'Now here it goes.' We were shocked when you suddenly changed your attitude and sat down calmly, receiving their blows. Then we realized that you are a brave man, a man of courage and willpower. Those tough students looked small compared to you. We respect you and are proud of you."

The news of that incident spread quickly through the school, among the faculty as well as the students. My English teacher and a number of students began to come to church. He and several students were baptized and became good church members.

7

To Surrender or
Not to Surrender

Another great change occurred in my life when I was twenty years old: I was drafted into the army. That was in the year 1926. The army was already in the process of the moral disintegration which took place between the Russo-Japanese War and the time of Pearl Harbor.

I think perhaps I should take time here to explain in some detail the composition of the Japanese Army, its aims, as they appeared to me, and my attitude toward it. That attitude may make clearer my own state of mind later when my native country, Japan, and my adopted country, America, were locked in war.

In the first place, I did not enter the army in any great spirit of regret or feeling that I was being abused. I was a patriotic Japanese, although my patriotism was for the old, righteous Japan, not imperialistic Japan.

From my study of history I knew that the Japanese Army had been an army of noble purpose. When the Russo-Japanese War broke out, the army showed not only its spirit of patriotism but also its high moral standard.

I regarded General Nogi as the central figure of the once moral army of Japan. In his day the aim of the Japanese Army was the defense of the nation; there was no room in the spirit of that army for a philosophy of invasion and conquest. After I was drafted I discovered that had all changed. The invasion of China and the conquest of the other small nations of Asia were the dreams of the army I knew personally.

I expressed my views on this in a paper all soldiers were asked to write while we were in training. I wrote, "I respect General Nogi in the Meiji Era very much. He made the Japanese Army a moral army. Today I cannot find any general in Japan whom I can respect. Today we are taught how to die in the battlefield but are not taught how to live as faithful soldiers of the nation. Every Sunday many soldiers seek merriment in geisha houses, saying: 'Let's live in joy today; tomorrow we will die bravely in battle.' Such a spirit may bring disaster to the nation."

An officer who read my paper and did not like it called me before him. "Are you a communist?" he asked.

"No," I said, "I am a Christian."

Such was my attitude toward the army. I sincerely believe that an army is necessary for the defense of the nation. However, when its purpose becomes invasion and conquest, it is not acceptable in the sight of God. It will then bring nothing but suffering and disaster to the nation, to the people, and to the world. This sort of an attitude did not make my early days in the army easy.

Physical conditions in the military service were very good, better in many ways than I was accustomed to in civilian life. Food was better than the average for civilians. For breakfast we had rice, soya bean soup with vegetables, and Japanese pickles. For lunch we had rice and salted fish and pickles, which we took in aluminum containers and ate in the drill area. Salted fish, broiled, was easy to carry. When we had lunch in camp, we had food cooked in soy sauce to go with the rice. For supper we had rice, cooked fish or meat cooked with vegetables and pickles. Though it may seem an odd diet by American standards, we considered it good in quality and ample in quantity. I never heard any complaint about the army meals.

Uniforms, too, were good. They were warm and strong, and the dress uniforms were attractive. Shoes were good and strong (although, as I will show later, I had my own personal troubles with the shoes). Each soldier received three kinds of uniforms. The best grade we wore only on special occasions such as national holidays. The next we wore on Sunday when we left the camp. Uniforms in the third class were worn only for training periods. This uniform was strong but not very good-looking. We were also given three grades of shoes—best, good, and shoes just for training. These last were not much to look at but they were strong and durable.

Officers (from sublieutenant to colonel) had their own meals prepared in their homes. They brought lunch from home when we went out for training. If they had to stay in camp for some duty, they ate the same meals as the enlisted men.

Sergeants who lived in camp were also given the same food as the lower-grade enlisted men. Married sergeants had their meals prepared in their homes and brought the food with them.

The army pay was not as generous as the food and clothing. A private received really only a token sum, 3.5 yen a month. A corporal got five yen. A sergeant living in camp got twenty-five yen, while a married sergeant living at home got sixty-five yen. By way of comparison, a young policeman in my native town, just graduated from high school, was paid forty-five yen a month.

I do not know how much the officers were paid, but there was a saying about them: "A sublieutenant cannot support a wife. A lieutenant can support a wife but no children. A captain can support both wife and children."

Army discipline was strict. It was enforced more by the matter of "losing face," a concept which Americans find hard to understand, than by physical brutality. For example, the jail in the camp was not a rough place. To any decent soldier, however, even two days in the camp jail was a terrible thing because he lost face. Some soldiers actually committed suicide in jail. Some killed themselves after coming out. Each man was given an army record book to keep for the rest of his life. Imprisonment was written in red ink in this book; other records were in black ink. A good soldier felt a deep shame over having red ink in his army record book.

I was the only Christian in my company of about 200 men. One of the sergeants gave me my first and most severe trouble.

He was a rough and uneducated man who hated Christianity. He really believed that Christianity was a devilish religion. When he found that I was a Christian, he considered it his duty to save me from this evil practice.

"Private Shimada," he told me once, "you cannot be a good soldier of the Emperor as long as you are a Christian. If you want to become a faithful soldier to the nation, you must give up Christianity."

I knew it was futile to argue with him about religion, so I tried to ignore him. He did not give up; he approached me again and again with the same old point. When he realized that I would not accept his advice, he used different tactics.

"Now this is an order," he said one day. "You must give up Christianity."

When he said, "This is an order," I had to obey it, or I had to make it clear to him that there could be no such legitimate order as "give up Christianity."

"Sir," I said, "I have read the army drill book. All proper orders are in the drill book, and I know that no officer can give any other orders than those written in the book. Would you please tell me on what page of the book I can find the order 'give up Christianity'?"

He did not reply for a moment, and I thought perhaps I had won. I could not have been more wrong. I am told that in the United States Army there is a saying: "They cannot make you do it but they can make you wish you had." The sergeant had something like this in mind.

"All right," he said, "if you do not accept our sincere advice but choose to keep the devilish religion, we will do everything in our power to make you give it up. Remember, this is the army, not a church. We have all kinds of advantages."

I realized that I had probably gone too far, but what choice did I have? I could not surrender on a point like that at any cost. I had to go to the end of the line.

"I know what you mean, and I am ready," I snapped back.

I should not have uttered such sharp words, but they came out before I could control them. I have always had difficulty subduing my fighting spirit in such a situation. When I have had time to reflect, I can be meek and humble, but on the spur of the moment my temper sometimes gets the better of me.

The sergeant was angry and was determined to show his superiority. Bayonet drill gave him a good opportunity to persecute me openly, making it look as though he were only doing his duty. He took full advantage of this chance.

Practically every morning all the soldiers practiced bayonet fencing for an hour. We did not use real bayonets, but imitations made of wood which were somewhat lighter than real ones, though of the same size and length. We wore iron face protectors like those we wore for fencing with a foil, but they were much heavier and stronger. We wore protectors made of some sort of heavy and strong material around the breast and trunk.

In spite of these protectors the bayonet fighting was a serious, deadly business. Several soldiers in other companies were severely injured during the practice and went to the army hospital. One of them died in the hospital; one of them became a cripple. These were accidents in the course of normal training; the danger became very much greater when the participants were trying to do each other serious injury.

In the beginning I was not good at bayonet fencing. For one thing, the protectors were too heavy for me, and it took a long time to adjust myself to them. This was probably not my most serious handicap, since in high school I had been called a "swift horse," meaning that I ran fast, I jumped high, and I was almost like a monkey on the gymnastic iron bars. Fencing should not have been too difficult for me. My real problem was that the idea of practicing to kill a man kept me from putting my whole effort into it.

The sergeant, on the other hand, was an expert with the bayonet. He moved about as if he were as light as a feather even with the heavy protectors. This was his chance for revenge, or to break my spirit.

"I will teach you how to fight with a bayonet," he said.

When he attacked me after this, I thought that three bayonets were coming at me. One seemed to be attacking my neck, another my chest, and still another my body, all at the same time. I could not tell which bayonet would attack me first and which next. I was a clay pigeon to him. He pretended that it was fencing practice, but he really attacked with his full power and skill. I was quite sure that he was trying to kill me. If this happened, he would not be blamed too much because it would be just an accident. His pointed bayonet seemed to be shouting to me, "Are you still keeping Christianity or are you ready to surrender?"

Every morning before the daily routine began, I said to myself, *This might be the last day of my life on earth. I must live like a true Christian.*

One day during the practice session he struck me so hard in the chest that I fainted. One of my comrades poured water on my face, and I came to my senses. The sergeant ordered me to stand up and finish the practice. I just did not have the power to rise; I was almost dead. I realized then that the situation was getting worse.

One of my comrades came to me that night and gave me some well-meant advice. "Private Shimada, you will be killed some day. You are fighting a hopeless war. Tell that sergeant you have given up Christianity and pretend that you aren't a Christian while you are here in the army camp. When you are discharged from the army, you can pick it up again. That's easy and simple. Why can't you do that? Be smart and fool that dumb sergeant."

This man really wanted to help me, but I could not do it that way. "Thank you," I said, "but you do not know Christianity. To me it is life. Without it I am as good as dead. You cannot throw away your life and pick it up again at a later time. Life is not like that. To give up Christianity means death to me. That's why I have to keep it. Please don't worry about me. I will find some means of protecting myself from his bayonet."

That night I gave some long, hard thought to the situation. I was in the army; I was trying to be a good soldier. Bayonet drill was part of a soldier's training. Why could I not bring myself to learn it, doing the best I could, so long as I did it in the spirit of fair sportsmanship and not in any revengeful or murderous frame of mind? I decided that I would regard it as a game and do my best. Attack, always attack, was the rule of fencing with a bayonet. Very well, I would attack. It would in any event be better than just waiting to be killed.

I had a good sleep that night. The next morning when I put on all the protectors, they did not seem to me to be so heavy. I tried moving around; I felt quite comfortable. When the sergeant came in, I went to him before he ordered me to come. I was sure I had become a "swift horse" once again.

That was the way it worked out. When we took the positions, I detected certain weaknesses in his fencing form. I jumped at him with a shout. I made it a savage shout, as we were supposed to do. My bayonet struck his chest so hard that he slumped back, abashed and surprised. At that moment he was in no position to fight back, and I could easily have attacked him and done him serious injury. Instead, since I was not angry but just doing my best in the game of bayonet fencing, I stopped and waited until he was able to take his regular position.

This time he came at me determined to fight with all the skill he had. The moment he started to charge, I quickly dodged his bayonet. He attacked air, staggered, and again his chest was wide open. He lost the fight completely. That morning I learned the secret of bayonet fighting.

Soon after that I was recognized as the number one bayonet fighter in the company. No one could successfully attack me, while I could attack and defeat any sergeant or officer.

During the critical three months it took me to pass through this ordeal I was literally fighting a life and death battle. The experience gave me the strong conviction that a man need not compromise his Christian principles to achieve final victory in any situation in human life.

While this struggle with the bayonet drill was going on I had another problem. It was not so serious, not a matter of life or death, but it was awkward for me all the same. It had to do with shoes.

The sergeant in charge of the clothing—suits, shirts, shoes, and so forth—was not so bad as the bayonet instructor, but he was always trying to get money from the soldiers. Those who came from rich families bribed him to receive better equipment. I had neither the money nor the desire to spend it for such a purpose.

One day this sergeant gave twenty-two pairs of shoes to our squad of twenty-two soldiers. He just dumped them in a pile. When the sergeant left the room, all the men rushed to the pile, trying to get the best-looking shoes. I did not rush, for this was all very trivial to me. I was quite sure that one pair would be left after all the others picked theirs. I was right, there was one pair left.

However, it was not really so simple. That pair of shoes was the biggest of the lot, and I happened to be the smallest soldier. They were much too big for my feet. I took them to the sergeant.

"Sir, this pair of shoes is too big for my feet. Would you please exchange them for a small size?"

The sergeant entered his storeroom. I hoped he would bring another pair, but he evidently was expecting money from me, and he waited for me in his storeroom where no one was watching. I knew what was on his mind, but I could not do such a thing.

When the sergeant realized that he could not get any money from me, he came out and said in a rough manner, "No, there was not a suitable pair for you. Go back with this pair."

"But sir, they are too big for my feet."

"Then make your feet fit the shoes, you fool," was his final answer. And he went away.

How could I make my feet fit those shoes? I had never heard such a silly thing in my life. But I had no other choice except to go back with my big shoes.

I asked a corporal in the squad room, "Sir, would you please teach me how I can make my feet fit this pair of big shoes?"

"Well, put three pairs of socks on your feet and put lots of newspaper in your shoes," he said. "That will do for a while, anyway."

I did as he told me and went out to the training field with the other soldiers. I was very uncomfortable. That day our training included jumping over a ditch with a rifle and heavy knapsack on our backs. It was not a wide ditch, and it was not deep either. Everybody could jump over. I thought I could do it easily too, but unfortunately I was very clumsy in my king-size shoes. I ran as fast as I could and jumped but could not get to the other side. I fell into the ditch.

"Private Shimada, is there any damage?" the sergeant shouted.

I thought he was asking me whether I was hurt or not. I just couldn't think of anything else when he asked "any damage?" I answered rather happily, "Sir, please do not worry. I am not hurt at all."

"You fool," he shouted, "I'm not asking about you. What about your rifle?"

I should not have been surprised. Soldiers had a saying: "Soldier is a penny-and-a-half, rifle is fifteen yen (1000 times more), horse is 150 yen," When a young Japanese was drafted, he was sent a draft card with a one-and-one-half cent stamp. For that reason it was common for a soldier to be called "One-penny-and-a-half."

There was also a saying in the army: "A rifle is more important than a soldier because the rifle is the symbol of the fighting spirit of the army. Any damage to the rifle means damage to the army spirit." Ridiculous though it was, the rifle was actually considered more important than the body of the soldier.

When I climbed out of the ditch, the sergeant examined my rifle from top to bottom. "You are lucky this time," he said. "If you damage any part of your rifle, you will be put in the army jail. Understand?"

"Yes, sir, I will be very careful, sir," I said.

The whole thing did not make sense. The smallest soldier, given the biggest shoes, was handicapped and fell into a ditch. Next time I would be put in the army jail. Yet I could not make any effective complaint. What a miserable life it was.

On the way back from the training field to the camp rain began to fall. Roads and streets became muddy. The newspaper in my shoes got soaked, and my feet were slipping around in the wet mess. I had a difficult time keeping myself from stumbling over my own feet.

I gave this matter some thought as well. I obviously would not get anywhere complaining about the damage to myself from falling in the ditch. I was only worth a penny-and-a-half. On the other hand, I could play their own game. That rifle was important. It cost fifteen yen; it represented the spirit of the army. It was clearly my duty to preserve it. Since I had already complained to the sergeant, with no result, it was not out of order for me to appeal to higher authority.

When we came back to the camp, I went to the lieutenant

and showed him my shoes with the wet newspapers.

"Sir," I said, "I fell into the ditch miserably, but if I could get shoes to fit, I am sure I can jump over that ditch. The sergeant did not have shoes to fit me. Personally I don't mind falling into the ditch again, but I certainly don't want to damage my rifle, sir."

"All right," the lieutenant said, "I will do something about it." And he called the sergeant. An hour later the sergeant gave me a pair of shoes that fit.

The next day I jumped over the ditch like a dog, climbed a high wall like a monkey, and ran around the training field like a horse. The lieutenant was satisfied with my improvement.

And so I gradually learned the ways of the army and how to adapt myself to them without compromising my principles. In time I came to be regarded as an excellent soldier, one worthy of promotion and a career. I will describe that in detail later, since it brought me face to face with another momentous decision and put great material temptation in my path.

8

The Japanese Army Finally Outwits Me

My life in the army settled into a regular routine. There was another sergeant who did not like me, but he did me no particular harm.

His primary duty was to be in charge of the weapons—rifles, swords, bullets, and other things. He had another job, however, which he enjoyed more. On Sundays all the soldiers received their passes from this sergeant. Without a pass a man could not leave the camp. Most of them wanted to go; this was, in fact, a soldier's only privilege.

However, two men had to remain in the company on Sundays, one as a guard and one to be on fire duty. This sergeant had the power to pick the two unfortunate ones for these chores. Partly because he disliked Christians, and partly because I never took him to a *geisha* house or bribed him in other ways as most of the men did, he often chose me.

This did not bother me as much as he thought because I did not have the money to spend on trips outside camp. I was giving my small allowance to my youngest brother, Takeo, for his education. I did not mind staying in the camp, where I could have a quiet time reading the Bible and praying.

I must admit, however, that I did not spend all my time in such worthwhile pursuits. I would not be giving a true picture of my army experiences unless I tell about some of my less praiseworthy activities.

One Sunday I was alone in the company area. I was sweeping the front yard when suddenly a horse galloped toward me.

No officer was riding him, and I didn't know how he came to be there. I tied him to a tree in front of the barracks. Then temptation began to get the better of me. I wanted to ride that horse.

I knew well enough that a horse was considered the most important thing in the army. I had not forgotten "soldier is a penny-and-a-half, rifle is fifteen yen, horse is 150 yen." I also knew the regulation that no soldier, except specially trained ones, could ride any horse in the army. I had never been on a horse in my life.

Still, I was tempted to give it a try. That horse looked so friendly and seemed to invite me for a ride. I untied him and mounted. I was a little frightened, so I held the reins tightly. The horse started to move backwards. I was more frightened, so I held the reins tighter, and the horse moved back even more. I wanted to make him go forward, but I did not know how.

Disgusted at that stupid horse, I kicked him. Then I really had a problem. He started to run while I, frightened and excited, could think of nothing better than to hang on and shout, "No, no! Stop! Stop!"

A major appeared in front of me and seized the reins. I did not know where the major came from or how he happened to be there. I certainly was not expecting any high-ranking officer like him in the camp on Sunday, but unfortunately there he was.

"Hey, you, one-penny-and-a-half," he shouted. "What are you doing on a horse?"

The major held the horse and waited for my explanation. This was a critical moment. I could not say that I wanted to ride a horse for fun. If I said so, I could certainly be imprisoned.

"Well, sir," I said, "this horse was running around here alone. I caught him and am trying to take him to the stable before he runs away somewhere else." It was about half truth and half lie.

"Oh, I see. Then it is all right. Get off. I will tie the horse here. You go to the stable and tell the soldier in charge about this horse. He will take care of it. Anyway, you are not allowed to ride a horse. Understand?"

"Yes, sir, I understand, sir. I will run to the stable right away, sir."

I got off the horse and ran to the stable. That was a narrow escape! Probably better than I deserved.

Another Sunday I was again on duty, and there was actually nothing to do in the camp. However, on that particular day a new bath house was opened for the Third Battalion to which our company belonged. A soldier in charge was going back and forth between the boiler house and the new bath house.

I looked inside. It was new, clean and attractive. There was plenty of hot water in the bathtub. The tub was big enough for fifty soldiers. It looked like an indoor swimming pool. I was tempted to swim there. A few minutes later I found myself swimming like a fish, having a grand time.

The next room was the officers' bathroom. I looked inside. It was smaller but much more attractive. I had no business to be there at all, but without any deep thought I promoted myself to considerably higher rank and made myself at home in the officers' bathtub. It felt great. I started to sing some hymns. At first I was singing softly, but by and by my voice rose to a crescendo, and it was soon at full volume. Just then an officer of another company appeared.

"Why are you taking a bath in the officers' bathtub? Explain!" He was really shouting at me.

"Yes, sir," I said, thinking hard. This was going to be tough to get out of. "This is the day when our new beautiful bathhouse is first open for use. The soldier in charge is very busy, going back and forth, checking this and that. He has no time to check the hot water and condition of air circulation in the officers' bathroom. I volunteered to check up on conditions. That is all, sir."

I thought it was a good explanation, except that it did not have the virtue of being even half true.

"Oh, I see. Then it's all right. By the way, how does it feel? All right?"

"Very good, sir, except for the air circulation. The windows may be too small in the summertime."

"Is that so? Perhaps we better put in an extra window before summer comes." With these words he left.

So that was another narrow escape. I decided I had better not sing any more hymns in the army camp, even on Sundays.

The sergeants were not the only ones who tried to win me away from my Christian faith and practices. Even my fellow soldiers tried, although I do not think they meant any particular harm by it. It was a game to them.

One Sunday while I was changing into a Sunday uniform, a comrade came to me and said, "I will take you to a wonderful place which is like a paradise, and I will pay for whatever you order there. How does that sound?"

It sounded fine. "What is it, anyway?" I asked.

"Well, you know what I mean. I'm talking about a geisha house. I know the most beautiful geisha girl in town. I will fix it for her to entertain you this afternoon. What do you say?"

"Nothing doing. I must go to church," I said.

The next Sunday another comrade came to me and offered the same generous invitation. He was a little more clever than the first. He said that he would come to church with me in the morning and in return I must go to the geisha house with him. I refused. The next Sunday still another one approached me with the same old story. By that time I realized that something fishy was going on.

"Tell me the truth. You are cooking something, aren't you? What is it?" I asked the third one.

"Well," he confessed, "we decided to invite you to a first-class geisha house and treat you to the best geisha and the most delicious dinner."

"It is certainly very nice of you, but what is the idea, anyway?" I asked.

"We know you have never been in a geisha house. We think you are missing something very important in life, and we want to educate you and make you a real man."

"Oh, I see. Now I understand why you invited me," I said dryly. "Thank you for your consideration, but I'm not interested in such an education."

Later I discovered that if a soldier had succeeded in taking me to the geisha house, he would have received a grand prize of money that a group of soldiers had put up. They had formed a lottery.

Since the term "geisha" is understood by Americans to mean many things, perhaps I should explain just what was meant by this lottery my comrades were promoting for my benefit.

Before World War II, whatever the situation may be today, there was no clearcut line between geisha girls and prostitutes. Of course, everybody knew the difference between the high-class geisha girls, who were supposed only to sing, dance, and play musical instruments according to the wishes of the customer, and the low-class prostitutes. There were, however, many who were between the two groups. In many cities geisha girls and prostitutes lived in the same area and often in the same houses. They dressed alike. People could not tell the difference, so they called all of them geisha. During the daytime a geisha house area was a ghost town. At night it was booming. Sunday was the exception. On Sunday afternoon the geisha house section was flooded with soldiers.

It was, therefore, no innocent amusement that my friends were offering me. They finally gave up the idea. I think they had more respect for me because of my attitude.

I should not give the impression that I did not try my conscientious best to obey the rules of the army and become a good soldier. I did try and was recognized by my superiors to the extent that they promoted me to corporal. This led to another incident in which I broke the regulations, but an incident which I still do not regret.

Usually the commander of the guard was a sergeant, but once in a while a corporal was used as a substitute. One day I was put in charge of fifteen guards for twenty-four hours.

I took over the duty at 8 A.M. It did not seem difficult. Men were on guard at the gates and all important places. I sat at the desk in the guard house, changing the guards every hour and keeping the place in order. I had a bugler who was supposed to blow for roll call at 9 P.M. and again at 6 A.M. for rising. His job was even easier than mine.

All through the day no problems arose. Everything went smoothly. At two minutes before roll call I ordered the bugler to get ready. At that moment a soldier ran into the guard house. He showed me his special pass. The pass called for him to be back by 8:45 P.M. He was almost thirteen minutes late.

In the Japanese Army this was a serious business. As commander of the guard it was my duty to put him in jail. He was late; there was no such thing as an excuse for being late. I have already explained how very tragic a thing it was for a Japanese soldier to be put in jail.

This man had not been drinking. His face was wet with perspiration, and he seemed agitated. The special pass itself showed that the situation was unusual. There was no time to ask him a question; I had to make a split-second decision. My heart pushed me to the side of leniency, although I knew that if I did not follow regulations and was caught, I would be imprisoned myself.

"Hurry back to your company," I said sharply. "Tell your officer that you reached the gate just in time. Don't say anything else. Understand?"

"Yes, sir." When the soldier saluted me his eyes were full of tears. He ran like a deer.

I ordered the bugler to wait, and I turned back the clock in the guard house ten minutes. I saw the anxious, worried faces of the guards. I was nervous too.

Then the telephone rang. It was a woman's voice. "Did my son reach there in time?"

"Yes, just in time. Was anything wrong at home?" I asked.

"Yes, his father is seriously ill. My son came back this morning with a special pass and was taking care of his father. Before he knew it, it was much later than we thought. But I am glad he was in time."

I ordered the bugler to proceed, and the roll call started. When the camp became silent and quiet again, I corrected the clock and spoke to the guards.

"I know I broke the regulations. This can be a serious matter for me. I may be imprisoned if one of you reports this incident to an officer. But as far as my conscience is concerned, I do not feel that I did anything wrong. I helped a soldier whose father is ill. I am glad I saved him. If that soldier were you, I would do the same thing. I know the army regulations are very important, but sometimes a warm heart is more important than any rule. I hope you keep this incident in your hearts and do not tell anyone until we are all discharged from the army."

The guards all agreed and promised to keep it a secret. They must have kept their promises for I was not imprisoned. Today, it is one of the happiest memories of my army life.

Some of the incidents I have told about may sound as though I always outwitted the army, but this was by no means the case. I can recall one episode in which I could have been in very serious trouble and which I got out of through the kindness of my captain rather than any wit on my part.

A historic army maneuver was announced for early in September of my first year in the army. All the companies of our Seventh Regiment were to take part, along with many others. We were all excited because the maneuvers were to be held at the foot of Mt. Fuji. This mountain is an inspiration to Japanese of all ages; we had all heard from our childhood of this beautiful, majestic mountain, which was the subject of many pictures as well as the source of countless poems, songs, and stories. Yes, Mt. Fuji was the sweetheart of all Japanese.

Strange to say, none of the men in our company had ever seen Mt. Fuji, and we were extremely excited. The importance of the maneuver was imposing, too. It was to be the largest in the history of the Japanese Army and would last longer than any other maneuver had ever lasted.

The announcement was made early in June, and training started immediately. We were all very anxious that our company show up well in the face of the stiff competition it would meet.

The training was not especially difficult, but it was different from our usual routine. We were taught to handle a high-angle gun, a strange weapon to us. We were taught to throw grenades into machine gun emplacements, to fight with gas masks on, and to cut and jump over barbed wire defenses. We learned to dig trenches under enemy machine gun fire, a hard task because it had to be done lying down. We were not even allowed to sit upright until the trenches were deep enough to hide us.

One evening in July, after supper, we were told that the next day the regimental commander himself would inspect our training maneuvers. We were ordered to do our very best, not only for ourselves but for the sake of the company. We were full of enthusiasm, cleaning our weapons and making thorough preparations.

The next morning, while we were getting into training uniforms, we realized that it was going to be a very hot day. Even so early the heat was oppressive. A splendid idea came to me. I would leave off my undershirt and wear my uniform directly over my naked body. We were supposed to wear undershirts at all times, even at night, but it seemed a silly rule to me, and I did not give it much thought. I certainly felt cooler that way.

The companies were assembled on the training ground. After a short instruction from the regimental adjutant we all— about 2000 of us—began to dig trenches under simulated enemy fire. We worked for two hours, and while the ground was not so hard here as we had expected, it was still hot, exhausting work. I congratulated myself on my wisdom in leaving off the undershirt.

The colonel of the regiment inspected our work and seemed satisfied; he ordered us to stop. After a thirty-minute rest he ordered all of us to make a semicircle around him and told the adjutant to give us information and instructions in regard to the Mt. Fuji maneuvers.

The adjutant seemed proud and haughty as he stood before us. His first words were a shock; he ordered all of us to take off our coats. I suppose he was only trying to be considerate and make us comfortable, but it was a bolt from the blue to me.

I didn't know what to do. All around me the soldiers were taking off their coats, while I sat motionless, trying to hide myself behind those in front of me. It did me no good at all; the adjutant noticed me at once.

"You, there," he called. "You—soldier in the coat. Didn't you hear my order? Take off that coat!"

There was nothing else for me to do. With the eyes of the entire regiment watching me, I slowly and reluctantly removed my coat and stood there as the only one among 2000 men not wearing an undershirt. I knew everyone considered me the most foolish and stupid soldier in the whole army, and I agreed with them. I was deeply ashamed of myself.

The next thing to happen was even worse than I had imagined. The adjutant ordered me to give my full name and also the full name of the captain of my company. I gave my own name in a loud voice, but when I was forced to speak the captain's name, my voice became very small. He was standing near me at the time. I saw him clench his teeth, his face pale. It was a terrible and undeserved disgrace for him.

"I could not hear the name of the captain," the adjutant shouted. "Say it again in a loud voice."

I had no choice. Asking the captain's forgiveness in my heart, I gave his name in a big voice. I felt terrible.

I felt even worse when the adjutant scolded my captain in front of all those officers and soldiers. "Your daily training must be very bad," he said, "if it produces such a foolish soldier as this one."

I saw that the captain's eyes were full of tears of resentment and anger, and I did not blame him. I would have felt better if he had struck my face with his hand a thousand times.

During the rest of the day's training I could think of nothing but my foolish error, which had resulted in consequences so much more disastrous than I had imagined. The adjutant talked to us about the coming maneuver, and we practiced fighting against tanks, throwing pint bottles of water that in reality would have been gasoline.

I was unable to concentrate on any of it. I knew my punishment would be serious, but that was not my prime concern. I worried most about how I could make up for disgracing the captain and the company.

I even considered hara-kiri, but that would have been an additional disgrace to the captain. I could think of nothing suitable by way of making amends.

The march back to camp, usually so joyful to all the soldiers, was to me like a march of death. My comrades let me know what they thought in no uncertain terms.

"What a disgrace; you dishonored the whole company."

"It was quite a one-man show. What a fool you are."

"You brought shame on all of us."

I tried to apologize, but my comrades did not accept the apology. I did not blame them because I knew it would be a long time before we heard the last of that incident. And I was 100 percent responsible.

Back in camp the corporal of my squad ordered me to clean up the barracks with a mop within thirty minutes, a job that usually took one man an hour. I got it done within the assigned time. Then he made me shine twenty pairs of shoes for the second-year soldiers in the company, again giving me less time than the job would normally take. After that I had to clean ten rifles in an hour.

He certainly piled the jobs on. I had no time to take a deep breath. I felt that I had no right to complain because I deserved all of this and more.

Then the sergeant of the week ordered the company to gather in front of the captain's office to listen to a special announcement. I expected the captain himself to pronounce a severe punishment on me that would be a lesson to all.

By this time I was calm and resigned to my fate. The captain, however, did not appear. He must have gone home with a heavy heart. The sergeant did the talking.

"Private Shimada dishonored the company in the presence of the entire regiment," the sergeant said. "I myself was so angry with him that I recommended a two-day imprisonment as a punishment. The captain, however, is going to think up some other punishment for Private Shimada."

Then the sergeant glared hard at all of us as only a sergeant could glare.

"Remove all coats," he said. "We will see if we have any other fools in the company."

I wanted the ground to reach out and swallow me up. I should have put on my undershirt immediately upon our return to the barracks, but I had been so busy with one rush job after another that I had completely forgotten it. Again I stood there, the only man with a naked chest.

I really expected the sergeant to jump at me and beat me, but he only stood there for a moment with his mouth open in surprise. I guess he was so astounded that he could think of no suitable words or action.

"*O-o-baka-yaro!*" he finally roared, meaning "You big idiot!"

Then he dismissed the company without another word to me or anyone else. He must have thought I was utterly hopeless and not worth bothering about.

That night I did not have the courage to pray. I felt that even God must be disgusted with me. I wondered if I really were a fool.

I heard nothing more of the incident except the comments of my comrades for about a week. Then the final rating of all the soldiers in the company was posted on the bulletin board. My name was the very next to the last. That was my punishment, but what a mild one it was. There was even one man lower than I, a dumb soldier who could understand "forward march" and "face backward," but who could not tell left from right.

I could feel the warm heart of the captain in this punishment. Imprisonment would have been written in red ink in my soldier's book, and I would have had no chance of promotion. That was the unwritten law of the army.

I determined to show my appreciation for his kindness by becoming a good and faithful soldier, not for my own sake but to make up to the captain the wrong I had done him.

9

The Captain and I

This captain was a man who showed me that the spirit of nobility and self-sacrifice was not entirely gone from the Japanese Army. He was not a Christian; he disliked and distrusted Christianity as much as any of the others. He was nevertheless a wonderful human being, with most of the character traits I regard as Christian.

Another incident involving him will further illustrate my point. Our company spent all afternoon under the hot sun of the sandy training field. We were exhausted, and the water from our canteens was all gone. We suffered from thirst on the march back to the camp. When we came to a shady spot under a clump of trees, the captain gave us a ten-minute rest.

We looked around for water, but not even a house was in sight. A farmer hauling a load of juicy fruits passed by in his wagon. The soldiers stopped him, and some bought the fruit. I did not have any money; so I didn't buy anything, but I saw no wrong in eating the fruit during our break.

The captain did not notice what was going on for a while because he was looking ahead through his binoculars and making plans. When he turned around and saw us, he became very angry. He ran up to the soldiers who were eating and shouted, "Attention!"

Everyone jumped to attention. The captain was so enraged that he lost control of himself and could not speak for a few moments. When he did speak his voice was terrible.

"You are still under army rules. 'At ease' does not mean that you are released from the army to become civilians. Your actions are unforgivable. No soldier in any country would do such a thing during training hours. When we return to camp, all of those who bought fruit will be severely punished."

The soldiers were frightened. They had not realized they were so seriously violating army rules. They marched back to the camp in silence.

When we were back in camp, standing in formation before the captain to wait for his verdict, he surprised us again by the warmth with which he addressed us.

"I told you I would punish you," he said, "but I am now beginning to realize it was all my fault. I failed to train you sufficiently in military rules. This time, and this time only, I will take the whole responsibility and punish myself. Attention! Company dismissed!"

The soldiers were so happy that they started shouting and talking among themselves. I was much impressed. I did not see how the captain could really punish himself, but it took a big and generous man to acknowledge publicly a fault in this fashion.

I was on night watch for an hour a little after midnight that same night. As I walked from one room to another in the company area, I noticed that the light in the captain's office was still on. Since he usually returned home at night, I thought he had forgotten the light.

I opened the door and was astonished to see the captain sitting in a chair. He sat there immovable as a rock, facing toward the southeast, his expression deadly serious. He did not turn when I came in. I saluted him, but he paid no attention to me.

I realized that this honest, conscientious man was doing just as he had told us he would do. He was punishing himself for what he considered the sin of the company. He was facing toward the Emperor in Tokyo, asking forgiveness for his fault. According to his views and the teachings of his conscience, the captain was a faithful servant of the Emperor. I told myself that I must continue to try to serve Christ in fully as faithful a manner.

From that moment I truly respected my captain. He was a sincere, dedicated individual, devoting his life to the things he considered right and just.

The captain also gradually began to have some respect for me and the manner in which I lived according to my beliefs. Approximately a year after I was drafted, three other comrades and I were promoted to corporal. About that time the captain permitted me to read the Bible in camp and showed me other marks of esteem. He got into the habit of calling me to his office and asking my opinion about various problems in the company.

One thing the captain discussed with me was the promotion of the enlisted men. Normally, promotions were determined by a group composed of the captain, one lieutenant, two sub-lieutenants, four sergeant-majors, and six sergeants. The sergeants knew the soldiers better than the others did because each had twenty-five men under him in his squad. In practice, therefore, the sergeants had more voice than the others in the promotion conferences because they had firsthand knowledge. However, the captain had the authority to make the final decision.

Each sergeant quite naturally wanted to get more and better promotions for his squad. Some sergeants tried to promote men not because they were worthy but because of some favor they had done for the sergeant. It was usual for the soldiers to give them money or gifts. Some took them to geisha houses on Sundays. This sort of thing happened more or less openly. If the men did not do the favors personally, their fathers gave the sergeants money or other gifts, hoping to advance their sons in the army.

The captain knew all these things, but he could not do much about it. It was a problem throughout the Japanese Army. If the captain were too strict about the bribery, the sergeants would not cooperate and the captain himself would be in trouble when the company was inspected during maneuvers. This would make him miss his chance of promotion. The captain, therefore, could not ignore the recommendations of the sergeants, but he wanted to be as fair as possible.

Thus he sometimes called me to his office unofficially and asked my opinion about the tentative list of soldiers to be promoted, asking especially about good men who might have been overlooked. He did me the honor of believing I would give him an unprejudiced opinion, and I always tried to do so.

On one occasion I found the name of a good soldier missing from the list. I told the captain that this man was a faithful and dependable soldier and that if his name were left off the list, the other comrades would be disappointed. I saw other names of those who were not worthy to be promoted, but I did not say anything about them. It was beyond my power to drop their names from the list, and I was not asked about them. When the list came out, the name I suggested was included in the promotions. No one knew the story except the captain and me.

Another time a soldier fell down during the training and broke the wooden part of his rifle. It was purely an accident and not the result of carelessness or neglect. The captain called me to his office and told me that he considered it his duty to punish this man. He asked for my opinion.

I said that it was not fair to punish a man for something that was entirely an accident. He had no intention of breaking the rifle and had not been doing anything wrong when he did so.

"I knew you would feel that way," the captain said. "If he had spoiled his uniform or shoes or practically anything else, I would agree with you and not pay any attention to it. The rifle is different; it is the symbol of the army spirit. Accident or not, a good soldier has to take the responsibility for a broken rifle. I have no choice but to punish him."

"Then why don't you give him a simple sort of punishment? A month confinement, perhaps." (This would have restricted the man to camp and denied him the privilege of going out even on Sundays.)

"No, that kind of thing is not punishment. Punishment means imprisonment. I must put him in jail."

I could talk freely with this captain. That was the purpose for which he had called me in. He knew that I would speak frankly but not presume on the relationship in other ways. I said, "If you have already made up your mind about the punishment, why have you asked my opinion? I thought there was still some possibility of changing your mind."

"No, there is no room for change. It has to be jail. I called you because I am afraid he might commit suicide. If he does, I would be in an embarrassing situation."

The captain said "embarrassing," but he meant much more than that. He meant that the matter would fall heavily on his conscience. I knew that with the soldier in question suicide was a real danger.

"Why don't you forget the whole thing and give him a new rifle?" I asked. "That would be easy enough to do."

"No, I cannot do that. This matter of the broken rifle must be reported to the colonel. I cannot say in my report that it was just an accident. I have to say that such an incident in my company shows that the spirit of the company is not high enough. I must take responsibility for this, and I must add that I have punished the man who broke the rifle."

I could understand his position. Within the framework of army policy and procedure there was really nothing else for him to do.

"I see how it is," I said. "I believe you want me to comfort him and watch him closely so that he will not disappear and commit suicide."

The captain nodded.

The next day my comrade was put in jail. Two days later he came back, looking pale. I tried to persuade him that it was not so bad, that he must have a "big heart," blow the gloomy feeling away, and start a new life.

That night I asked eight volunteers to watch him closely every moment during the night. I made a schedule, with each of us watching him for an hour. We kept this up for three days and nights until I came to the conclusion that the danger of suicide was past.

I reported this to the captain, who deeply appreciated our efforts.

After I had been with the company for a year and four months, the captain called me to his office for an entirely different type of discussion. To my great surprise, he proposed that I remain in the army as a career and become an officer. He said that he had not liked me at first because he considered me a "sissy" Christian, but that during the first year he had discovered that I had guts, energy, and a tremendous fighting spirit. He was sure I would make a good officer.

He had the program all planned. He told me that he had an opportunity to send one of his sergeants or corporals to the army training school within a year. Such a chance was a great honor, one that came to the company only once in many years. He wanted to give that rare chance to me, hoping that after two years of training I would come back to his company as a lieutenant.

It is hard to convey exactly, in this time and place, what a wonderful opportunity this was for me, what a coveted avenue for material advancement it offered.

Today few young men even in Japan have any great desire to become an army officer. However, before World War II, practically all capable young men were ambitious to be officers. Military men were very popular among the people. Young ladies hoped to become the brides of young army officers, and their mothers were eager that their daughters become officers' wives.

Well, I was not particularly interested in young ladies, but I was ambitious. I also had dreamed of being an army officer in uniform. Before this interview such a thing had been entirely beyond my reach. It was not easy at all for a young man to pass the entrance examination of the officers' school. Almost all the top students from high schools all over Japan tried to enter the school. Only about one out of every hundred of these applicants had a chance to get in.

Since I was not a top student in high school and since I had no way to pay the cost of the school, it had been hopeless for me. My father was so poor that I could not expect to go any further than high school unless I received a good scholarship. Thus, I had given up the hope of becoming an army officer and became a bank clerk when I finished high school.

Now the captain was opening the way for me, removing all obstacles. I would not need to pass any examination except the physical and some oral tests. I did not have to worry about expense either because the company would take care of that.

When the captain offered me that rare chance, I thought to myself that this might be my golden opportunity; this might be a reward God was giving me.

"Thank you very much," I said. "Please give me two days to

consult my father and relatives."

"All right," he answered, "I will wait for two days, but no longer. Don't let me down."

The next day I received special permission to go out. I went to my father first and asked his opinion.

"It's a good chance," he said. "Don't miss it; accept right away. I want you to become a great general some day." He was more excited than I was.

Even my aunt, who was a rich farmer's widow but a stingy aunt, was enthusiastic. "If you become an army officer, it would bring honor to us all," she said. "If you need money for this, I will be glad to help you."

I talked it over with some of my best friends. All of them encouraged me to accept that wonderful offer. Their opinions were unanimous. I came back to the camp with a cheerful heart. The evening meal was an ordinary supper, yet it tasted like a banquet to me.

Night approached. The roll call was over, and all the soldiers went to bed. I could not sleep because I was so excited. I was imagining my future as an army officer. I visualized a nice-looking young lieutenant, then a captain, then a major. My dream promotions were so fast that within a few minutes I was the top general of the Japanese Army of three million soldiers. I had the largest building in Tokyo as my headquarters. I was sitting behind a big desk in my room. Several generals and I were looking at a map of Asia.

"Gentlemen," I said, "our territory is from Siberia to Java, and from China to the Marshall Islands. This huge territory will be ours." All the generals agreed with me. I was the genius of the group. I felt great. I was the ruler of Asia.

While I was in the midst of the ecstasy of my military dream, I heard a small voice in my heart say, "You big fool!" The voice was so strong and clear that my glorious dream was shattered completely, and I was a corporal again in a hurry.

"You big fool," the voice continued. "Your foolishness is larger than the whole of Asia. You know it is written in the Bible ' . . . all they that take the sword shall perish with the sword'; yet you are trying to become a military man. Do you think that the Bible is mistaken in this particular teaching? Do you think you would be an exception because you would be a Christian militarist? All the Japanese militarists in uniforms are great heroes in your eyes, but in the sight of God they are withering flowers. If you take the sword and become a military man, ignoring the warning of the Bible, some day you will regret it in agony, and your agony will be forever. If you become a servant of God, not only will you be blessed, but your family and many other people will also be blessed through you.

"You know that this army of which you dream is not an army of peaceful defense; you know it is an army of conquest and ruin.

"You are at the crossroad in your life. You have asked for human advice but forgot to ask God's opinion. This is the time for you to shut your ears to all the human voices and listen only to God's voice. This is the time for you to close your eyes to all the earthly glories and look up to the heavenly glories. You are here in the army camp not to become a military man but to become a servant of God; you are here not to learn militarism but to learn to bear persecutions for the sake of the gospel. Don't choose the foolish way, but take up the cross."

The voice was too strong for me. I tried to ignore it, but I could not. I tried to evade it, but it followed me like my own shadow. Yet I did not want to give up that golden opportunity. I was indeed standing at the crossroad, and my struggle continued until dawn. Finally I surrendered to God and prayed, "Father, let thy will be done."

It was my Gethsemane. That temptation was the greatest one in my life. I will be eternally grateful that, with God's help, I managed to overcome it.

In the morning, before the daily routine training began, I went to the captain. "Sir," I said, "I thank you very much for your kind offer, but after deep consideration I have decided not to become an army officer. You see, I have to become a servant of God. That is God's order."

"I did not know you were so foolish," he said. He seemed deeply disappointed. "I did not know you were influenced that much by Christianity."

In spite of my rejection of his offer, this wonderful man

never changed his friendly attitude toward me. Several days later he called me to his office again and talked to me, not as a captain but as one friend to another.

"Mr. Shimada," he said, "I believe you are ready to die for Christ, just as I am ready to die for the Emperor. I can appreciate your spirit, but I just cannot understand why a man like you cannot have the same attitude toward the Emperor. Jesus Christ was a Jew who died long ago, but the Emperor is a Japanese and is living now. Don't you think that it is better to die for the living Emperor than for a dead person? I just cannot understand that point. Do you really believe that Jesus Christ is greater than the Emperor, who is the living god?"

I knew he was not trying to trap me with this question. (During World War II many Christians, especially ministers, were trapped in such a manner. Those who answered that Jesus was greater than the Emperor were called traitors and were imprisoned. Many of them were forced to answer that the Emperor, the living god, was greater than Jesus Christ.) When my captain asked this same question, he was really trying to understand my point of view.

"I respect the Emperor as the father of the Japanese people, and I salute him in this spirit," I said. "But I worship Christ as the Divine Being. To compare the Emperor with Jesus Christ is a mistake."

"But we believe that the Emperor is the divine and living god. Do you deny that?"

It was a difficult question for any Japanese Christian to answer before the war.

"You and I are using the same words," I said, "such as 'divine being' and 'living god,' but the meanings are entirely different. When I say 'God,' I mean the Creator of the universe, the Creator of all human beings; when you speak of the Emperor as the divine and living god, you do not mean that the Emperor created heaven and earth and is the creator of all human beings."

"That's right," he said, "I do not mean it that way. I simply mean that the Emperor is the greatest person and the ruler of all Japanese people. In that sense I call him a living god."

"In that sense," I said, "the Emperor is still a human being to me."

The captain could not understand that point. The Japanese people regard many national heroes as divine beings. Admiral Togo, the hero of the naval battle of the Japanese Sea during the Russo-Japan War, was promoted to divinity by the people. In the same way General Nogi became a god. In Japan, people are the creators of gods.

The captain was, after all, a typical Japanese. It was impossible to make him understand that Jesus Christ is the only begotten Son of God and the true Divine Being. We arrived at a deadlock. He realized that it was an uncomfortable discussion. He changed the subject and spoke kindly.

"If there is anything I can do for you in your preparation for the ministry, please let me know. I will try to do it for you."

"There is one thing," I said. "If I could be discharged from the army six months early, I would be able to enter theological school in September of this year."

"Well, that is a difficult request," he said, "but let me study it, and if there is any possibility, I will try. Anyway, I will let you know about it in a month."

I knew it was a big request and beyond his personal authority. I thought it was a good chance to ask, but I did not really expect it to work out.

A month later the captain called me to his office. He smiled as he showed me a piece of paper. It was his letter of recommendation for my early discharge. I will always remember one sentence in the captain's letter: "Corporal Shimada is the most faithful and sincere soldier to the nation I ever saw."

There were five signatures on the letter. The first was the captain's own signature as company commander; the second, that of the battalion commander; the third, that of the regimental commander; the fourth, the brigade commander; the last was that of the divisional commander himself.

"With the agreement of these five commanders," the captain said, "you are going to be discharged from the army on the 10th of July. This is a gift to you from me, not as your commander but as your friend."

And so I learned that not all good men are Christians. This captain was one of the finest men I ever knew. I have since tried to determine whether he is still alive, but I can find no record of him. I suppose that he was killed somewhere in China during the war.

I am sure that he died doing his duty as his conscience permitted him to see it.

10

The Treacherous Son

I find it difficult to make my American friends understand the exact nature of the relationship between father and son among the Japanese people, particularly the responsibilities of an elder son. A father's word was not only the law to a good son, but it was such a son's duty and pleasure to have it so. Traditionally, the eldest son was supposed to remain at home and look after his parents. Younger brothers had no such duty. To go against the wishes of a father, particularly a kind and loving father, even though the son felt those wishes to be entirely wrong, was a tragic thing.

What followed now in my life was therefore a shattering experience for me. I felt I was impelled by a force stronger than any personal wish. I dreaded the effect what I had to do would have on my father. It was my duty to please and obey him in all things. That was the teaching of the culture in which I was raised; it was also my personal wish. And yet in this instance I knew that I could not do so.

My father had remarried while I was in the army. My sister was already married, and my brother Masashi had gone to Osaka to work. The home, with only my brother Takeo and my father left, was a lonesome place. He no longer felt it his duty to remain a widower.

My stepmother was a simple woman with no schooling. She could not even write her name. She was a widow who had never had any children and wanted to marry a man with good children. She was good-natured and friendly.

It was an arranged marriage, of course. They were brought together in a relative's home and decided to marry. Both were lonesome. A few days later the ceremony took place. My father was forty-seven at the time, my stepmother forty-one.

My father was disappointed when I was discharged from the army. He had hoped very much that I would stay and become an officer. He had, however, respected my wishes and not really ordered me to do so. He tried to hide his regret.

"What are you going to do from now on?" he asked. "Are you going back to your old job in the bank, or are you going into some business?"

I could think of no way to soften the blow. I knew that what I had to say was going to be a much greater shock to him than my decision to leave the army.

"I want to become a Christian minister, Father," I said. "Would you please give me your permission?"

His reaction was just what I feared it would be. He was startled and shocked beyond description.

"Wait a minute!" he shouted. "You are my first son. You must stay at home. You have to think of your family and your community. It would be all right to go into the army, where you would bring honor to us all. This is a different thing entirely. If you were my second or third son, I would not care so much whether you wanted to become a Christian minister or a Buddhist priest. But since you are my first son, you have a responsibility and duty to take care of the family. I am getting old. Within a few years I have to retire from my work and must depend on you.

"I want you to give up Christianity and come back to our family religion. It's perfectly all right for you to study Christianity as your hobby, but I warn you not to go too far. Our family religion has been Buddhism for a long, long time. I cannot change it, and you cannot change it either. Whether you like Buddhism or not, you have to be faithful to our family religion."

He was very serious. I had never seen him so serious, nor so upset over anything, in all my life. I asked him for three days to think it over. I knew I could not change my decision, but I hoped that during those three days some way might be shown me that would enable me to soften his opposition. He agreed to the delay.

In the days that followed I thought and prayed, trying to discover a magic formula for making him understand my faith and see my point of view. I loved and respected my father. I did not want to make him unhappy. It had been my sincere hope to be his good son throughout my life, but the situation was impossible. I could not fulfill both the orders of my heavenly Father and those of my earthly father at the same time. No miracle came to me.

At the end of the three days, which flew by much too fast, I went to my father again.

"Father," I said, "after much thought and prayer, I have come to the same conclusion. I *must* become a Christian minister. There is no other work for me. Please permit me to go to theological school. I will not ask you to help me financially for I believe I can take care of myself. I only ask your blessing."

"My son," he answered, "I may not have been a good father to you, but I have done my best for you and for my other children. Is it too much to ask you to stay home and take care of me?"

I could not reply for several moments. He was a loving father, a hard worker, and a dedicated school teacher. I could not expect a better father than he in the whole world. He had sacrificed the best ten years of his life for me and my brothers and sister. Now he was asking me to sacrifice a little for him. As far as he was concerned, it was quite a reasonable request. From the traditional standard of Japanese ethics he had a perfect right to expect me to remain at home, and I had no right to refuse. But I was no longer living in the old, traditional world. The new Christian world was opened wide before me.

"My father," I said, "you have been a wonderful, loving father to me, and I have been hoping and trying to be a good son. I believe I have never before disobeyed you. However, this time I cannot obey your orders because God ordered me to become a minister. I cannot go against God's will."

It was the best answer I could manage, but it did not help the situation at all. He was furiously angry.

"If your God orders you to go against your own father, then

your God is not good! He is a devil! Now I realize clearly that Christianity is an evil religion. Your God is trying to destroy a happy, innocent home; your God is actually taking a son away from a poor father. He is a devil, and you are a wicked son."

He was so lost in anger that he seemed almost crazy. He struck my back as hard as he could and shouted at me.

"You are no longer my son! Get out of my home and never come back! I will never forgive you!"

My stepmother began to cry and ran from the room.

He threw me out of the house. He disowned me. It was a terrible experience. Although I had feared this might happen, it was still a great blow. I felt as though my heart were broken. I lacked the strength to stand in front of the house; I sat down on the ground and wept in agony. I prayed, *Please take good care of my father while I am away from him. Someday I will lead him to Christianity, and baptize him with my own hand.*

It was a prayer, and it was also my promise to God. Yes, it was a covenant made between God and myself. After this prayer I received the strength to stand up and walk.

I was penniless and had nothing; I decided to go to my cousin and try to borrow some money. I had to go through the downtown area to get to his house. As I walked through the crowded streets, I felt as if I were walking alone in a dark forest. I was oblivious to the noise around me; I did not hear a sound. There was nothing but loneliness. I neither saw nor heard anything. I was thinking only of my poor father, who was also brokenhearted, believing that he had lost his son.

My cousin gave me a small amount of money, and I went to a Canadian missionary in Hamamatsu. The missionary, the Reverend Harper H. Coates, was kind and understanding. I stayed in Hamamatsu for several weeks, helping him and learning English from him.

My cousin wrote me that many people in my native town were saying that I was the worst son the city of Kanazawa ever had. Christianity had changed me to a treacherous and rebellious son. I had proved Christianity to be an evil religion.

When I read the letter, I said to myself, *Someday I will show them that I am a good son and that Christianity is the best religion in the world.*

11

A Trial Student

At the beginning of September, I went to the School of Theology in Kwansei Gakuin University with a letter of recommendation from Dr. Coates. I showed the dean of the school the letter and asked him to permit me to enroll. The dean was an American missionary named Dr. Hayden.

"You have a good letter of recommendation from one of our respected missionaries," the dean said, "but our school started in April, and this is the middle of the first semester. It will be better for you to come back next April, when you will be admitted."

I had expected some such discouraging answer and was prepared for it. I tried to speak calmly and reasonably.

"Yes, I know September is the middle of the semester. But it is God's order for me to become a minister, and this is the school of God, isn't it? You must allow me to enter; otherwise, all that has gone before does not make any sense. If you do not permit me to enter, I will go on a sit-down strike and will not move until death."

I realize that this method of procedure is open to criticism. The threat of a sit-down strike (this was a very well-known phrase in Japan at that time) was not a good method for a student who intended to be a minister. However, I could think of no other. I had no home to return to, no place to go. I do not even now regard my action as stubbornness; it was simply that my determination to study for the Christian ministry was overpoweringly strong.

I actually sat down on the entrance step of that school of God, waiting for their decision. I sat for hours. The dean called a special faculty meeting because of me.

I heard later that one of the professors asked the dean, "Don't you think he is a little bit off?"

"No, I don't think he is off," the dean said. "He seems all right to me. Just determined."

The professors decided that I might enroll as a trial student until the end of the first semester, and if I passed all the examinations, I would become a regular theological student. To me that seemed fair enough. I did not care whether I was a trial or regular student, just so I had a chance to prove how earnest I was. The unusual arrangement satisfied me.

I really studied diligently. In high school I had been about an average student. I did not study very hard, and Chinese literature and athletics were about the only courses that interested me. When I entered the seminary, my attitude was entirely changed. I was really a different person. I was strongly conscious of the fact that I had dedicated myself to God, and I regarded study in the school of theology as part of my mission.

Study of the Old Testament, the New Testament, church history, Greek, Hebrew, English, theology, philosophy, homiletics, and hymnology were all part of my preparation for becoming a servant of God. I even studied hard on the courses I did not care for.

When the examinations for the first semester came in the middle of October, I passed them all with rather good marks. The professors were surprised, and I was a little surprised too. The dean called me to his office.

"From now on," he said, "you are a regular student. I am glad to have you in our school. We have decided to give you a scholarship."

That was very good news. The scholarship, which covered room, board, and tuition, was more than I had expected. At least I did not need to worry about starvation. A Canadian professor in the literature department asked me to teach him the Japanese language for three hours a week. He paid me well, and that extra income covered all my other necessary expenses.

All the students in the school of theology were expected to help in various Sunday schools. The dean asked me to help in a certain Sunday school in an outcast community about fifteen miles from Kwansei Gakuin.

These so-called outcast communities are a peculiar institution in Japan. They began in the ancient time when many Chinese and Koreans migrated to Japan. They were not outcasts in the beginning; they were just newcomers. They did not mix with the Japanese, simply because their language, customs, manners, and foods were different. They generally established separate communities.

The newcomers ate the meat of cows and pigs. In the Japan of that day only the lowest classes ate meat; fish was the accepted food. Most Japanese believed that eaters of four-legged animals were unclean people and so began to look down on these newcomers.

After one of the civil wars some 800 years ago the survivors of the losing Heike clan hid themselves among these new communities. These survivors remained there for a long time; so that now the blood of these *samurai* is mixed with that of the early Chinese and Koreans.

We do not know just when they started to be treated as outcasts, but it began before the time of that long-ago civil war. About 100 years ago the government declared that the outcasts were new citizens of Japan, but the Japanese people did not accept them readily, and the outcasts did not try to mingle with the Japanese either.

The outcast group with which I was assigned to work had a Shinto (a purely Japanese religion) shrine built by the community people, which meant that this particular community had more Japanese than Chinese-Korean elements.

I found that our Sunday school was held under a tree in the Shinto shrine. No church was connected with that Sunday school. My school was more or less responsible for the religious instruction of the community.

The children were rough and tough. They knew they were outcasts, and they were full of resentment and were very sensitive about the discrimination. The theological student who had been in charge of the school before me quit after he was beaten by these children with their wooden clogs.

The community standard of living was very low. "Unsanitary" is inadequate to describe their living conditions. The dean explained the situation and asked me to take care of that Sunday school. He knew that I was a trained soldier and that I would not be afraid of the physical danger. I looked on the assignment as a challenge and accepted.

On my first Sunday the dean himself took me to the area and showed me the shrine and the place where the children were supposed to gather. A few children were playing in the yard of the shrine. They knew right away that we had come to see about their Sunday school. The dean introduced me to them, and I asked them to bring all their friends.

Soon about twenty children gathered under the tree and asked me to tell them an exciting story. I told them the story of Jesus in his boyhood days. I thought they might be interested in it and might be inspired by it. I was very wrong.

"Hey you, shut up," one of the boys said. "We don't want that sissy stuff. Don't you know any good stories?"

And so on that first Sunday I was a failure. The next week I went there quite early because I wanted to play with them. Several girls were there in a circle, playing a game. They did not pay any attention to me, although I had supposed them to be waiting for me; they just went on with the game. I stood and watched.

It seemed an ordinary game, but they played it very seriously, with no thought for their new young teacher. At the end each girl threw a few pennies on the ground, and one girl gathered them all up and put them in her pocket.

I was shocked, realizing that they were gambling. They did not seem to be ashamed of it at all even in front of their teacher. I begged them not to play this type of game anymore.

"This is none of your business," one girl said. "You better shut up or we'll clog you like we did that other guy. As long as you don't stick your nose into our business, we'll let you come to our shrine. Understand?"

She was really a rough girl. I had a tough group on my hands. That day I told them the story of David and Goliath, with big gestures and motions. They were all interested and listened intently. I thought I was on the right track, but my story backfired. Right after Sunday school the boys started a new game called "David and Goliath." At first it was just play, but it turned into a regular stone fight. I had a hard time trying to stop them. My talk had certainly inspired them all right. I was rather confused about how much good I was doing.

At the beginning of the new school year I volunteered to take care of this Sunday school for another year. By that time I had come to know all the fifty or so families in that outcast community. The head of the community began to like me, and one day he invited me to lunch after Sunday school.

I knew that if I refused his invitation, he would resent me, and my work there would become even more difficult. I accepted it as a challenge and went to his house for lunch.

When I arrived at the house, I was struck by a disagreeable odor. A very sick woman was lying in a very dirty house. I had to eat lunch with him in the same room where the sick woman lay. The rice bowl and chopsticks appeared never to have been washed. I lost my appetite from the very beginning, but I ate everything on the plate, pretending to enjoy it. He was very much pleased.

"We have had several Sunday school teachers," he said, "but you are the first one who accepted my invitation. You are all right. Whenever you have trouble, don't hesitate to come to me. I will help you."

One day a girl about twelve years old came to me, smiling and happy. "I am going to graduate from grade school next spring," she said, "and then my father will sell me to a geisha house, and I will become a geisha girl."

I was shocked. "I will talk to your father and the head of the community and save you from this. Don't worry."

"Why are you going to try to stop me?" the girl asked in astonishment.

"Why? It is a terrible thing to be sold. It is not right. I must stop it for your sake."

"Please don't stop me," she pleaded. "I want to be a geisha girl. That is my only dream and hope. All the other girls here want to be geisha girls, but they aren't as pretty as I am. They have no chance, but I am a very lucky girl; they envy me."

"You don't know anything about geisha girls," I said. "You will regret it when you realize what a geisha girl really has to do."

"I know everything about geisha girls," she said, "because others from here who did as I want to do came back and told us everything. I will like the life of a geisha. It is full of fun with men, and it's the easiest way to make money."

I was discouraged and deeply disappointed. I considered myself a failure because my services among these people for two years had brought no noticeable results. I lacked the courage to volunteer for the third year. I still wonder whether my work there did any good at all.

I do not regret leaving this task since my successor, who intended to be a social worker, was interested in the community and wanted the assignment. I do not know that he was any more successful than I, but he enjoyed his work more.

During my five years in Kwansei Gakuin I did not have much financial difficulty because of my scholarships and my teaching job. In my third year, however, there was no job available during the summer vacation. I stayed in the dormitory because it was most economical. I ate only twice a day, breakfast and supper. My meals for two months consisted mainly of rice and seaweed twice daily. It was economical, if nothing else.

During the next nine months of that third year I continued to go without lunch, even though it was not strictly necessary. I did it because I wanted something very much.

What I wanted were two sets of books that were held in the highest regard by seminary students majoring in the New Testament, as I was. They included a five-volume Bible dictionary, edited by James Hastings, and *The Great Texts of The Bible*, an even longer work, also by Mr. Hastings. The second-hand sets that I bought were far beyond my means, as my scholarship gave me only board, room, and tuition, and the Canadian whom I had been tutoring had returned to Canada. I had to take drastic measures.

The only means I had to pay for the books was to cut out my lunch, which I did for a full nine months. This wasn't easy; I was only two years out of the army where at least I had eaten well. At noon I just drank water and to forget my hunger went into the school chapel and sat at the reed organ.

I picked up a book on music fundamentals in a music room and "borrowed" it for a time. I had never taken music lessons, except the little taught in school. I learned to play the hymns by myself, one by one, until at the end of the year I had memorized the four hundred or so hymns in the Japanese hymnal. During my fourth year in the school I was made a chapel organist.

I completed the five-year study in the Kwansei Gakuin University School of Theology in 1933. The joint commencement exercises of all the departments were held in the central auditorium. About two thousand students and many guests were gathered there. The commencement started with the high school department, and other college departments followed, with the theological department the last. The dean of the seminary called my name and asked me to come forward.

I was overwhelmed as I found myself standing before an audience of two thousand students and distinguished guests while the dean honored me with a special certificate in recognition of the highest scholastic record since the school was founded forty years before. I felt a lump in my throat. I remembered that I had entered the seminary as a trial student five years earlier, and I was now leaving the school with the highest of honors. My heart was full of gratitude.

When I received the special certificate, I heard the thunderous applause of the people. It was one of the happiest moments in my life. Still I felt a certain sadness, for there was not a relative to share the joy with me.

My covenant to convert and baptize my father remained unfulfilled.

12

A Green Pastor

At the annual conference of the Methodist Church in Japan, I was accepted as a trial minister. This was the same as being a trial student; all theological school graduates were "trial ministers" in the beginning.

I had expected to be appointed to a church in Kyushu, the southern island of Japan, because I had received an invitation from that church, and I had given them an affirmative answer. Instead, I was appointed to a small church in Osaka. The church itself was suitable for a green young pastor, but Osaka was something else again. An experienced and mature minister would normally have been placed there. I learned that the dean of the school of theology asked the bishop to appoint me to the Osaka church.

There were some reasons for his request. Officially, the dean was hoping to send me to America within a year or so for further study. On my return he planned to make me a professor in the school of theology. It would be much more convenient for me to remain close to him.

There was another reason, not so official, of which I had been aware for some time. The dean had a marriageable daughter. He also had a capable son and another daughter, but the son, whom he had wanted to follow him into the ministry, went into business instead. It was natural enough for him to want his daughter to marry a minister. It was also perfectly natural, and in keeping with Japanese custom, for him to attempt to arrange the marriage.

I had known the dean had this in mind since my senior year. I can recall the first time he had me to dinner, although to tell the truth I remember the food from that incident better than I remember the girl. It was a *sukiyaki* dinner, which the dean himself cooked at the table on a small charcoal burner. He was very good at making sukiyaki. It was a memorable treat for a poor student.

The dean's daughter was an attractive, pleasant girl, who played the piano beautifully. After dinner she played some hymns while the dean and I sang together. The dean sang the melody and I the bass; sometimes the girl sang alto. It was all very pleasant.

I was invited to dinner several times after that; both the daughter and I knew what was in her father's mind. I liked her, but more as a sister, and I don't believe she had any particular desire to marry me either. We were just friends. The dean, however, continued to make his plans.

I have personally always felt strongly opposed to an arranged marriage, at least for myself. It is not that I am against traditional customs or ideas. I am perfectly willing to keep good ones, and I do not believe in trying something just because it is new, either. My philosophy is to accept what is best from both the old and the new. As far as I was concerned, the arranged marriage was definitely one of the old traditions I did not care to keep.

I first made this resolve about the time I went into the army when my sister was married. All was arranged in the typical Japanese way. My father and the boy's parents settled everything, and one day a young man came to the home of one of my relatives and met my sister. The next day there was a simple wedding ceremony. I considered it so strange and unnatural that I decided I would never accept an arranged marriage.

It is my conviction that finding a wife is like finding a treasure. It is a privilege and an adventure to find the treasure for myself; accepting even the same treasure, if one could imagine such good fortune, found by someone else would not be so meaningful.

The arranged marriage has by no means died out in Japan, although at present a compromise way is popular. Parents select the future bride with the help of a go-between (usually a married couple who knows both families); and the young people meet. They are given a period in which to get better acquainted, usually a few months. Then they can decide for themselves, but in most cases they get married. This method is not entirely new; it was practiced to some extent before the war, though it is more popular now. To me it is not much better than the old system since it still carries the spirit of the arranged marriage. The purpose of giving them this period is not to see whether or not they love each other. The purpose is to let them get to know each other better; in most cases marriage is expected by the parents. The parents still believe that love comes after marriage.

The dean, however, did not know my views on arranged marriages; so I was assigned to the church in Osaka.

I went to the appointed church with hope and faith. It was a very small church indeed, with the chapel downstairs and the parsonage above it. There were only about twenty people in the congregation, but when all twenty came to the morning service, the chapel seemed full of people.

I was not a complete success in my first church. A few of the older members stopped coming to church because I was too young and did not have the ministerial dignity they desired. They said I had a boyish face. Perhaps they would have preferred a more dignified, sour expression. On the other hand, several young ladies started coming for the first time; so as far as numbers went, I kept about the same average.

Living alone in the parsonage was inconvenient, and I had no intention of getting married. I asked my younger brother, Takeo, to leave our native town and live with me in Osaka. He consented and moved there. Fortunately he got a teaching position in a public school near my church. On Sundays he helped in my Sunday school.

In September a hurricane hit the Osaka area. Some parts of the city were struck by a tidal wave, and two of my church members, a mother and her twenty-five-year-old son, lost everything. House, clothing, furniture, everything was carried away by the water. They were left alive but had no place to go.

I invited them to live with my brother and me in the parsonage. It really worked out very well. The mother cooked and kept house for us, which was most convenient. We lived that way until I came to America.

I stayed and preached in this small church for two years. In the meantime Japan was becoming more and more militaristic. A military policeman started to check my sermons. He came to my parsonage and warned me that I had better watch what I said. Frequently on Sundays he came to the church services in a civilian suit and stood there, very recognizable for what he was, checking my sermon. Sunday morning services quickly dropped in attendance. The evening services were also lonesome. I became very discouraged.

I was pleased when, through the dean of the school of theology, I finally was given the opportunity to go to America for further study. I felt that it was a good thing for me to do while Japan was under military control.

The Southern Methodist University School of Theology (the name was later changed to Perkins School of Theology) offered me the scholarship I described earlier. I have also told how friends and church members raised money for me to make the trip.

When it became known that I was to leave for America for further study, the Reverend Kugimiya, who later became the bishop of the Methodist Church in Japan, advised me not to marry a *nisei* (second-generation Japanese-American). He was afraid that I might not return to Japan if I married a Japanese-American. Several days before my departure the Reverend Nakamura, superintendent of the Osaka-Kobe area of the Methodist Church, came to me and said, "I know a fine young lady. I want you to marry her before you go to America."

He did not mention a name, but I knew she was the daughter of the dean.

"I have no intention of getting married now," I said. "I want to be perfectly free while I am studying in America."

"If you do not want to be married now, it would be a good idea to be engaged to her. This is a very good chance for you."

"Yes, I know," I said, "but I have to stay in America for five years to complete my studies. Something unexpected may happen to me or to her during the coming five years. No one knows. I do not think that it is a good idea for us to be engaged and restricted for five years."

The superintendent finally accepted my position and departed. I knew she was no more eager to be married than I was. In the end it all worked out for the best. About six months later this girl married a minister; so perhaps the dean was satisfied after all.

I sent a letter of congratulations from America. And I remained free to search for my treasure in my own way.

13
"Texas, Here I Come!"

I have already told of my problems with the Immigration Service and how they were solved. Now at long last my dream was realized; I was in the United States of America. I was a very happy man.

I arrived in San Pedro in the spring, and the school did not open until fall. This time I was not so impetuous as when I staged my sit-down strike at the theological school in Japan. I planned to remain in Los Angeles, where there was a substantial Japanese community, until school started.

This Los Angeles period was important to me in that it let me meet Mr. Nobe, one of the unforgettable characters of my life. He was a member of the Japanese Methodist Church in Los Angeles.

He was a man of seventy-five who was a total stranger to me. He heard about me and invited me to stay in his house. No one has ever been more kind to me.

Mr. Nobe had three sons and three daughters, four of whom were married and living in lovely homes in Los Angeles. He would have been welcome in any of those homes. However, he liked to live all by himself, although every evening he visited one of his children and had dinner with the family. These visits were his chief joy, but he refused to live with any of them.

While I was staying at Mr. Nobe's house, the minister of his church went to Japan to visit his father. He planned to remain in Japan for three months. The church members asked me to take the place of their minister while I was in Los Angeles. I gladly accepted their invitation and served as a substitute minister during June, July, and August.

Mr. Nobe was very pleased about it. He began to be busy caring for me. He insisted on preparing lunch for me every day even though he himself did not eat lunch. Every evening he took me to one of his sons' or daughters' houses for dinner.

Mr. Nobe liked to sing hymns although he could not sing well. He was always somewhat off key. I taught him many hymns, but I could not teach him to carry a tune. He also asked me questions about the Bible, and I helped him to understand the meaning of many Bible stories.

He was young in heart and spirit. "I feel as if you were my own father," I told him once.

"Oh, that's bad, that's awfully bad, that's bad indeed," he said.

"Why is it so bad?"

"Because," he said, "I want you to feel as if I were your brother."

Soon after that he started to work for two or three hours in a shoe repair shop near his house. I tried to discourage him and advised him to stop working. He was, after all, seventy-five years old.

But he said that he needed a little money for a good cause, and every morning he went to work and came back home a little before noon to prepare lunch for me.

One day he asked me to go to the cemetery with him and see his tombstone. "You mean your wife's tombstone?" I asked.

"No," he said. "I want you to see my own tombstone."

I went to the Evergreen Cemetery with him, and there I saw a new tombstone with his name on it. He asked me to sing a hymn about the eternal life. I sang one or two, and he joined me in singing. He was off key, of course, but that did not detract from his joy.

"Mr. Shimada," he said, "whenever I come here and sing a hymn, my heart is inspired and filled with thanksgiving, and low, earthly desires disappear from my heart. Today I am especially inspired and strengthened by your singing."

The month of August passed, and when I was about ready to leave for school, Mr. Nobe gave me thirty dollars. "This is a small gift to you," he said. "I have been working to save this for you. Please accept it for school expenses."

I was speechless. I had no idea that this old man had started to work again to help a student like me. I will always remember his kindness. He passed away when he was ninety-four years old.

And then, at long last, I was on my way to Texas.

When I was in high school in Japan, I often saw movies of Texas cowboys. I loved the vast plains of Texas and the cowboys galloping freely through the prairies. Texas had been my dreamland when I was young.

This youthful sentiment came back, and I said, "Texas, here I come, whether you like it or not; you have been my dream, and I hope to be somebody to you."

Southern Methodist University in Dallas had a quiet and spacious campus, just as I had expected. The School of Theology of S. M. U. was just the right size for me. It was not too large and not too small. I felt at home in the school. At least I did not feel that I was lost. Dean Hawk, a fatherly man, was the one who had made the scholarship possible for me. I expressed my deep appreciation for his kindness as soon as I met him.

I plunged immediately into my studies, which were difficult for me because of my problems with the English language. My first grades were not as good as I had hoped, but I realized that the language handicap made it necessary for me to study even harder, and I did so. I was always optimistic and thoroughly enjoyed my school life.

Professor Davis, under whom I studied the New Testament and New Testament Greek, spoke so fast that I frequently could not follow him.

Dr. Hicks, the Old Testament professor, was even more difficult for me to understand. Some of the students told me that Dr. Hicks had studied the Hebrew language for so long that even his English had a Hebrew accent. I don't know the truth of that, but it certainly was not a Japanese accent.

I also studied church history and theology under Professor Goodloe. He was a profound thinker and a man of deep faith. I loved his sermons more than his lectures. There was also Dr.

Root, who gave me good marks on my papers in sociology and comparative religions. And there was Dr. Seneker, who gave me deservedly bad marks in religious education, which was a course I did not study hard enough.

The worst mark I ever received was an "F" from Dean Hawk in a test on wedding procedure. My point of view was that I had come to America to study the Bible and theology, not wedding procedure. Whether the bride or the groom came first seemed entirely unimportant to me.

I had performed two wedding ceremonies in Osaka before coming to America, and both were very simple because I arranged them that way. I do not like fussy, elaborate things. I am not interested in formality. "Simplicity and dignity" is my motto in life.

In my Osaka weddings, therefore, I just asked the bride and groom to stand in front of me, while the guests and relatives were seated. I read the Christian ritual, not in a ritualistic tone but as if I were talking personally to them. I did not like some of the words in the Japanese ritual; so I changed them to more simple terms.

Such was my view of weddings. Uniting the man and woman in holy matrimony before God and the people, that was the important part. I felt that was all that was necessary in Japan, and since I did not intend to remain in America, I saw no sense in wasting my time on all the fussy things necessary for an elaborate American wedding.

I definitely do not recommend that young ministers follow my example. I soon realized that I could not expect Americans to accept my way of conducting a wedding and that I would have to adjust to their way.

However, I have been unusually fortunate in that this ignorance of procedure did not greatly handicap me; my wife has always taken care of all of the details. She is a perfectionist, who has to have things just so. She takes full responsibility for instructing the wedding party, attending to the bride's wishes, and so forth. My part—to me, the important part—is the ritual. God blessed me with a wife who meets my every need, and I am always grateful for this blessing.

I can still remember the first wedding I performed in America. It took place about a year after I was married. It went very well although to my mind it was overly elaborate. After giving the final word of benediction I shook hands with the bride and groom congratulating them. Then came a custom for which my wife had not prepared me.

Right there in public, before the eyes of the minister and the congregation, the groom kissed the bride! I was so shocked that I almost fainted.

My wife assured me later that it was the American custom, and quite all right. Now, although I have learned to stand and endure this through more than 100 ceremonies, I still don't feel comfortable about it.

(Before the war American movies shown in Japan were censored, and the kissing scenes were cut out before they were shown to the public. Now even the movies made in Japan, with Japanese actors and actresses, have extreme love scenes, including kissing.)

My wife often laughs at me because I get so nervous when the bride approaches me step by step in the procession. I am always worried about how she is going to look. This stems from an experience in another early wedding in Alameda. During the rehearsal the bride-to-be's hair was fixed in a most peculiar style. I thought it must be fixed up specially for the wedding and was probably an "American custom," but it looked terrible to me. The next day as she came down the aisle during the procession, she was so beautiful that it made me terribly nervous. I did not see how a woman could change so much in appearance overnight.

Later my wife told me that the bride-to-be's hair was set in something called pin curls during the rehearsal, so it would look nice the next day. I don't know what my wife did to her hair, but I was glad that I had never seen *her* in pin curls.

Aside from the bad grade in wedding procedure, the only trouble I had in S. M. U. during the first year was with the food. I thought I liked American food, but it seemed that I liked only Japanese versions of American food. During that first year I suffered acutely from "food-sickness" rather than the usual "homesickness."

I could not acquire a taste for butter, cheese, milk, or coffee.

I wanted rice and salt fish, but such things were not to be had either in the dormitory dining room or in any restaurant in town. There was ample food in America, but I could not enjoy it. Whenever I went into the dining room, the same old smell killed my appetite. Every night I dreamed of a heaping bowl of steaming rice and a ten-pound salt fish.

The only things that agreed with my stomach were potato chips and Coca-Cola, which I had for breakfast every morning for several months.

I often sat alone under a tree on the campus and meditated on rice and fish. I am sure I was usually given credit for more exalted thoughts.

One day a fellow student approached me and said, "I think you are homesick, and I don't blame you. What you need is a girl friend who can make you happy and cheerful."

I was not homesick because I had no home; I had been cast out from home long before. Since that time, wherever I went was home to me. But he was correct about one thing. I was sick, all right.

"By the way," he said, "a girl in another department here would like to be your girl friend. She thinks she could cheer you up and encourage you. She hinted to me that I should get your reaction. How do you like the idea? If you had a steady girl friend, your English conversation would improve. What do you say?"

I was intrigued. Improving my English conversation was certainly a high-minded reason for having a girl friend.
"Is she pretty?" I asked.
"Sure, very pretty."
I couldn't help being excited at the idea. "Suppose she were my girl friend, and I were her boy friend, what should I do?" I asked. I never had a girl friend, so naturally I did not know what to do with one.

"You have to take her to a restaurant and treat her to dinner once in a while, and at the same time you would learn English conversation and American etiquette."

"Oh, I see," I said. "Who would pay?"

"You have to pay, of course. It is a privilege for any boy to take a girl to dinner."

I thought to myself that it would be some privilege! While she enjoyed the American food I would be thinking about rice and salt fish.

My friend continued talking, not realizing my inner thoughts, "And then you have to take her to the movies often."

"Don't tell me I have to pay again."

"Certainly you have to pay. Don't be so stingy."

"No. I would try hard not to be stingy, but she sounds awfully expensive to me," I said.

"And when you walk with her on the sidewalk, you have to walk on the outside and let her walk on the inside."

"Why?"

"If a reckless driver comes along, you will be in the right position to protect her from danger."

"Well! The whole idea is certainly different from that in Japan. There the men are treated like kings."

He smiled and said, "This is not Japan. What is your answer?"

"Give me a day to think it over. I will have a definite answer for you tomorrow."

That night I considered whether I should have a girl friend or not. My thoughts ran this way: *I am perfectly free; I am not married; I am not engaged. In America having a girl friend is not a strange idea at all, and it will not look odd even if I walked hand in hand with her. This is America, not Japan. This is really a golden chance for me to improve my English conversation.*

Then there came another thought. *Suppose our friendship grew deeper, and we wanted to get married; then what would happen? She would have to go to Japan with me, and she might not be happy in a foreign country. She would become "food-sick" and homesick. Then it would be a tragedy for both of us. It is better for me not to have a steady Caucasian girl friend. I came to America to study the Bible, not to have a good time with a girl.*

The next day I gave my friend a negative answer.

"You had better meet her anyway," he said. "I am sure you would change your mind."

"That's what I am afraid of," I said. "Anyway, will you please convey my deep appreciation to her?"

"All right, I'll do that, but you are missing a good chance."

That was the end of the story, but even today sometimes I wonder what kind of a girl she was. Was she pretty? Was she slim or plump? What was her name? When I told my wife about this, she said, "You should have had her for your friend. She might have helped you with your English conversation." That was not at all the attitude I expected. My wife surprises me sometimes.

I did have one girl friend while in school. Soon after I decided against meeting the Caucasian girl, the theological school held a banquet. It was to be the first big social event of the year, and each student was to bring his wife, if married, or a date. I was sorry I had not accepted that girl friend, whoever she was, for now I had no one to take, and I wanted to go to the banquet to see what such an event was like in America.

I remembered then that when I left Japan for America, one of my church members in Osaka gave me a handsome rag doll as a present. "I am poor," she had said, "and have no money to give you. I made this doll. Would you please take her to America and remember me when you see her?"

This woman was a faithful Christian. She had four children to support. Every penny had to be used for her family. She could not afford to buy dolls for her children, so she made them. It was one of these dolls that she had given to me. It was not an attractive doll at all, and I was not interested in a doll anyway, but I appreciated my friend's sentiment. I brought the doll to America.

On the night of the banquet an idea came to me. I took the doll from my old suitcase and christened her "Miss Tokyo." My Miss Tokyo had a poor kimono, a homely face, and an unbalanced figure. She wasn't even worth being called "Miss Village." I took her to that big banquet and put her on the chair next to mine. My ticket included my date, so she had the right to occupy a seat.

The banquet started off with gaiety. When each student had introduced his wife or his date, I stood up and introduced my Miss Tokyo from Japan. My date received the biggest applause of all. I had a grand time with Miss Tokyo that evening.

I wrote to the woman who gave me the doll, telling her about the banquet and Miss Tokyo. In her answer she said she was so happy she would like to make a dozen "Miss Tokyos" and send them to me. I declined the offer, telling her that there should always be only one Miss Tokyo.

Perhaps this is a good place to explain that I have not spent all my years in America disliking American food. I like some of the food very much now. I have even at long last learned to drink coffee, although I like Japanese green tea better. I can drink a cup of coffee or two with sugar and cream anytime during the day, but I don't think I enjoy coffee as much as most Americans do. I will not touch coffee in the evening because it keeps me awake almost until midnight. Many friends have told me that this is a psychological matter. Psychological or not, it surely keeps me awake for a long time. When I drive a long distance, I often drink a cup of coffee to wake me up.

I like chicken the best of all American food. I like any kind of chicken now, but at first I hated to see it cooked with bones. This seemed savage to me. When I was in Japan, I never saw chicken cooked with bones. The meat was always cut into bite-sized pieces.

The first time I saw fried chicken piled on a platter on the table in a restaurant, I lost my appetite. Somehow the pieces reminded me of cooked human bodies. When I ate a piece of fried chicken, using knife and fork for the first time, I felt as if I were a barbarian. Here I was stabbing with a fork and cutting with a knife and eating chicken with bones. I did not feel good at all. I thought that using chopsticks for meals was much more refined.

I still do not care much for beef cooked in the American way. I prefer sukiyaki to a T-bone steak or roast beef. I like fish, fried or broiled or prepared in any way. Trout, salmon, and crab are my favorite seafood. I like almost any fish cooked in the American way, but of course, fish cooked in the Japanese style is still the best for me. I like pork cooked in the American way. I don't think I ever ate pork in Japan. Pork and turkey were not popular there when I was a young man.

Fruits and vegetables are fine. I liked them all from the very beginning except spinach. Spinach cooked in the American manner is not for me. I enjoy all kinds of fruit in America, especially grapefruit and seedless grapes.

Today I eat an American breakfast, a Japanese lunch (most of the time), and either an American or a Japanese dinner (about half and half). I have not acquired a taste for cheese. I really suffer when I am served macaroni and cheese.

One day shortly after arriving in Dallas I rode on a street car. There were not many people in the car. As I looked for a good seat, I noticed the sign "Colored" in the back section. I looked at my hand; it was yellowish brown, certainly not white. "Well, I have some kind of color, all right," I said to myself, and sat down in the colored section.

Soon after the car started running, the conductor saw me in the mirror. He stopped the car, came to me, and asked me to move to the other section. It was confusing. After that I always tried to find a seat as near the boundary line as possible.

I was not always identified as a Japanese in Texas. When I met Dr. C. C. Selecman, president of Southern Methodist University, for the first time on the campus, he asked, "Are you an American Indian?"

"No, sir, I am not," I said.

He did not ask any further questions, so the conversation ended there.

Three weeks later, on a Sunday, I was walking to the Highland Park Methodist Church. This time I was dressed in my best clothes. I met Dr. Selecman again.

"Are you Irish?" he asked.

"No, sir, I am not."

He shook his head and walked on without further comment.

I said to myself, *My goodness, within three weeks he has transformed me to an Irishman.*

Henry, one of my fellow theological students, was assisting in the First Methodist Church downtown. He asked me to give my testimony to his young people's group. I accepted his invitation.

He advised me to take a street car and gave me directions. "Tell the conductor, 'Please let me get off at St. Paul.' He will let you off at St. Paul, and I will meet you there and take you to the church."

So I took the street car and asked the conductor to let me off at St. Paul.

"All right, I will tell you when we get to St. Paul," he said, staring at my face. A little later he said, "Now this is St. Paul."

The stop was rather a dark place. I waited and waited there for an hour and thirty minutes, but no one came. In the meantime poor Henry was waiting for me at the other St. Paul in the downtown area. I was waiting at the St. Paul in the so-called Mexican area, which Henry did not know about. Evidently the conductor mistook me for a Mexican and let me off at the St. Paul where he thought I belonged.

I often wondered why I was so frequently mistaken for an American Indian, an Irishman, or a Mexican. I decided that I must have interracial traits.

One day when I was taking a train trip, I received a graphic illustration of the way I confused people. When I got on the train I saw a short, awkward-looking fellow on the opposite side. He looked to be American Indian or Mexican, or perhaps Chinese. He was rather poorly dressed. As I walked toward him, he walked toward me. When I stopped, he stopped. I realized that I was seeing myself reflected in the mirror placed on the door dividing the white and colored sections of the car. I was shocked; this was not the mental picture I carried of myself.

After thinking it over, I realized why I had not recognized myself immediately. I had never seen myself in a mirror except in a small shaving mirror, and while shaving I didn't bother to analyze my appearance. I had been living among those tall, handsome Texans for so long (many were rich and well-dressed at S. M. U.) that I must have subconsciously concluded that I had become a tall and handsome Texan, too. That train mirror showed me I was still just five-feet-three-inches tall.

I have been writing of these matters of race relations in a light vein because that was the way it appeared to me at the time. All of America was new to me. I met surprising and startling new customs on every hand. The racial discrimination did not make a deep impression on me, and I found my personal experiences humorous rather than shocking.

It was not long before I realized that the question of race

relations is one of the most serious problems America has to face. I am not an authority on this complicated problem; I have no easy answer to it. I believe that America is the greatest nation in the world, both today and throughout history, in economic, military, and political fields. I have hope and faith that in matters of race this great nation will also show the world she is not a backward nation.

14

First Summer Vacation in Santa Barbara

Near the end of the first school year I found that my money was practically gone. The immigration officer had been right; I needed more than $500 a year. I had to get a job during the summer vacation and save at least $200, or I would have a very difficult time getting through my second year. (I learned that the immigration law permitted a foreign student to work during summer vacation.) I asked several of my fellow students to try to find a job for me.

A week before the summer vacation began I got a letter from the Japanese Congregational Church in Santa Barbara, California, which solved my problem. The letter read in part: "Our Japanese church is a small church. We do not have a minister. Please come and spend your vacation here with us. We want you to preach in Japanese on Sundays and teach the Japanese language to our children on weekdays. The salary is $100 a month."

It was too good to believe; for a while I thought it was a dream. I accepted the invitation right away, and the day vacation started I took the train for Santa Barbara.

Even then I did not realize at first how very fortunate this appointment in Santa Barbara really was for me. I thought of it only as an opportunity to serve as a pastor and as a way to save money for the next school year. In reality, something much more significant and lasting came from that summer.

In Santa Barbara I was provided with a small apartment in the church building. I had to cook for myself, a thing I had never done. I bought some groceries at a small Japanese store near the church operated by Mr. and Mrs. Imai.

One of the first things I bought was a can of coffee. I did not like to drink coffee, but I thought that at least I should know how to make it in case I had visitors. I bought a can of coffee all right, but I did not know how to open it. There was an old-fashioned can opener in the church kitchen. I used it to make a small hole in the top of the lid and got the coffee out with a spoon.

I put three spoonfuls of coffee into hot water and waited for a while and drank it. I did not like it at all. Meantime Mrs. Imai, a member of my church, dropped in to see how I was getting along with the coffee. She laughed and laughed because I had opened the coffee can the Japanese way.

"Poor minister, you do not know anything," she said. "How can you cook?"

"Well, I can learn how to cook by experience, can't I?" I answered.

"You had better come to my house for every meal," she said. "I have to cook for my husband and myself anyway, so one more person won't make much difference."

I started to have my meals in Mrs. Imai's home, which was not far from the church. I always felt at ease there because they were friendly and kind. At that time I did not know that they had a lovely daughter, Nobuko, who was ill in a hospital in San Diego.

It was not long before Mr. and Mrs. Imai and I became good friends. They asked about my family in Japan. They often spoke affectionately of their twenty-four-year-old daughter and of her older brother, Yuji, who was working in San Francisco after his graduation from Stanford.

One day Mr. and Mrs. Imai told me that Nobuko had completely recovered and would be home soon. Naturally I was happy for them; I did not realize what it would mean to me.

In Japan I had pretended to be a woman-hater because that was the accepted code among Japanese boys. To seem interested in girls would cause a boy to be called a "sissy" and treated accordingly. Naturally, I pretended like the rest. My performance was so good that during my high school and college days my friends actually believed my act. Yet, deep in my heart, I was dreaming of a beautiful, young Christian woman, as any other young man would do.

I told myself that I must be very particular about my future wife because a minister's success depends largely upon his wife. If he has a good wife, he will be more successful in his ministry and will be able to do better service for Christ and his people. She should be a woman of deep faith and warm heart. She would be called on to sacrifice worldly position and many earthly things for Christ and the church.

There were of course many girls in Japan who possessed these qualities, but deep in my heart I knew that I was looking for something else as well. She must be someone I could love and want to spend the rest of my life with. I still did not believe that "love comes after marriage."

When I left Japan for America, I felt that I had put romantic dreams aside for the time being. I did not know much about Japanese communities in America, and I certainly did not expect to meet my dream girl in a foreign land beyond the Pacific Ocean. I did not even imagine meeting a Japanese girl in America.

The next day when I went as usual for lunch to the Imai's, a lovely girl opened the door for me. The sight of her left me speechless for a moment. She was beautiful. Somehow she reminded me of my young mother, whom I had always remembered as the most beautiful woman in the world. I had of course never seen my mother in American-style dress, but even in the different costume the resemblance was striking.

I felt a warm, happy feeling deep inside myself. I forgot everything for a moment and stood looking at her.

"Won't you please come in, Mr. Shimada?"

That awakened me from my dream. I went through the door, feeling as though I were entering a strange, unknown house.

"I have heard many nice things about you, Mr. Shimada," Nobuko said in Japanese. Not only was her Japanese correct, but her voice seemed sweet and beautiful to me.

"Thank you. I have also heard many people say Nobuko-san is a fine Christian lady," I said, also in Japanese. "How is it that you speak Japanese so beautifully?"

"I lived in Japan for three years as a child. I almost finished grade school there before I returned to America."

Nobuko and I soon became close friends; there was a bond that seemed to draw us together. She helped me with my English conversation and corrected my pronunciation. I in turn helped her with Japanese writing, for while she had continued her study of Japanese after returning to America and spoke the language almost perfectly, she had trouble writing some of the difficult letters.

She told me all about her life in Japan, where she had gone with her parents when she was eight years old and her brother Yuji was eleven. Her uncle, a prosperous exporter, had asked her father to come back and join him in the business.

Nobuko and her brother were interesting novelties to the Japanese children. English was a compulsory subject in the middle school (high school) and was very popular. The boys from a nearby high school (secondary schools were not co-educational in Japan before World War II) often surrounded Yuji to listen to his genuine English.

Nobuko also was often surrounded by people who wanted to hear her speak Japanese with her American accent. She said that after a week or so she was chattering like the neighborhood children in their dialect and had to relearn standard Japanese after coming back to America.

Yuji became more and more in demand among the high school students. They often came and asked to "borrow" Yuji for a time. They would take him with them to practice English and send him home with hands full of cookies and candy.

The English teacher in the boys' high school, a Japanese gentleman who had studied the language only in Japan and spoke with a strong accent, asked Yuji and Nobuko to speak to the class. Dressed in their best American clothes, they were taken to the high school by their uncle.

It was a large class of senior boys, all in uniform. The room was packed. The teacher introduced them by saying, "Today you will hear genuine English, imported from America."

Nobuko said that her brother had practiced his speech at home, using a loud, clear voice and emphasizing the proper points. Standing in front of that crowd of big boys he looked very small and nervous, and she was afraid that they would not be able to hear him.

She was not nervous, which surprises her now because she has grown much more timid about public appearances. As a child, however, she had no self-consciousness and did not feel the least embarrassment over reading her favorite story of the three little pigs and reciting "Little pig, little pig, let me come in."

Yuji adapted himself quickly to the new life in Japan, wearing Japanese clothes and soon being accepted as one of the group. Nobuko was unhappy at first. The girls in her school were not required to wear uniforms, and as she felt ill at ease in a kimono she wore her American clothes. The girls were friendly and she liked them, but the boys tormented her. They pulled her hair and threw pebbles at her. Whenever they saw her they shouted, "America, America." She began to dread recess. She remembered how polite the boys in her American school had been and was sorry that she had come to Japan.

She finally refused to go to school, and her mother went to see the principal about the situation. He called an assembly to talk with all the students about being kind to the new girl from America, and after that she never had any trouble.

"You just didn't understand the psychology of Japanese boys, Nobuko," I said. "They didn't tease you because they disliked you. They liked you and wanted to get your attention."

She told me about another incident that she remembered with embarrassment for many years. She was asked to be an angel in the Christmas tableau at the Congregational church which she attended. She told the minister's wife that she had an angel's costume she had brought from America. The woman was pleased and asked her to bring the costume with her to church the next Sunday.

Nobuko said that she was really confused. The dress was a fairy costume she had worn in a school program in America. It was made of pink crepe paper, with a short ballet skirt and glittering ornaments. There was even a crown and a wand.

"This is an angel's costume from America?" the minister's wife asked.

Nobuko assured her that it was. She had the angel and the fairy mixed up and badly wanted to wear the costume.

"Well, all right," the minister's wife said. She must have thought things were strange in America.

Nobuko excitedly told her uncle that she was to be an angel in the Christmas program. For some reason she did not tell her mother the exact part she was to play. Her uncle, who took a keen interest in his niece and nephew from America, was even more excited than Nobuko. He was not a Christian and was not familiar with the customs of the faith.

"I'll make you a pretty angel," he said, and helped her fix some of the ornaments that were coming off her costume. He wanted the costume to be in the best possible condition.

Nobuko said that it was many years before she could laugh at the picture she must have made in the manger scene, wearing that glittering pink fairy's costume, wand in hand, bending over the Christ child.

While in Japan Nobuko learned to play the *koto*, a zither harp about six feet in length with thirteen silk strings. (Now they are nylon strings and more durable.) It was played with three ivory plectrums.

I asked her to play the koto for me. She promised that she would on the following day, and when I arrived I found her wearing a Japanese kimono. To me she looked much prettier in the kimono than in American clothes.

When her fingers touched the strings of the koto, sweet Japanese music flowed out like the singing of spring birds. It also sounded like a stream, running at the foot of a mountain and in a deep forest.

"How do you like it?" she asked, smiling.

"Beautiful," I said. "Simply beautiful. I would like to hear more."

Nobuko had returned to America with her parents when the export business, in which her uncle and father had invested everything, went bankrupt. Nobuko was too young to understand what had happened, but she did realize the sudden change in their financial circumstances. Yuji was left in Japan for further study in Doshisha Institute, a Christian school in Kyoto.

She has never forgotten the thrilling experience of standing on the deck as the ship sailed into San Francisco Bay and the skyscrapers began to appear on the horizon. She felt she was really coming home to her own country. As she grew older and recalled this joyous experience, she could understand the sentiment of her parents at the first sight of the snow-capped peak of Mt. Fuji in early dawn on that morning their ship sailed into the harbor of Yokohama.

After she returned to America, she began to prefer the piano and then the pipe organ to the koto, and she practiced less and less on the koto and finally gave it up. The pipe organ was one of the things she loved most.

"Would you please play the pipe organ for me sometime?" I asked. She seemed pleased and promised to do so.

I really did not like pipe organ music. I had heard it for the first time at Southern Methodist University (there were only three pipe organs in all Japan at that time) and to me it was just a thundering noise. I often noticed in the church services that the organ music was so loud that the singing of the congregation was drowned out completely. Nevertheless, I wanted to please Nobuko and wanted to hear her play.

She and I went to a large Caucasian church, the First Presbyterian Church, where her teacher was the organist and where she took her lessons and did her daily practice. There were no other people in the large sanctuary when we arrived. She explained that the organ was a three-manual organ with two large rooms full of pipes.

When she sat at the organ, I was expecting that thundering big noise. To my surprise a soft, sweet music like that of the Japanese harp came from her fingers. At first I thought that her fingers were so small and tiny that the music had to be soft and sweet. But I was wrong. Suddenly the thundering storm came. I looked up at the ceiling, wondering if it would fall down upon us. When she finished the piece, I applauded heartily.

As the days went by our friendship became deeper. I realized that she was a woman of deep faith and of noble character. The more I knew her, the more I respected her and loved her. To me she was a perfect blending of the East and the West.

We often drove to a hilltop behind the city of Santa Barbara where a beautiful view of the city lay before our eyes. Whenever we came to the hilltop we somehow felt that we were closer to God, and our thoughts became purer. We sang Japanese and English hymns together on the mountain.

We also went to the seashore in the evening to see the great Pacific Ocean. We loved to watch the beautiful reflection of the moon upon the water. We especially loved to see the waves that dashed toward the rocks and spread into thousands of drops in the air. Jesus Christ, the eternal rock, was attacked by the waves of ungodly people for twenty centuries, but he was not destroyed. The waves, however, were shattered into pieces.

I was persecuted in high school, in the army, and at home, but my Christian faith was not broken. Nobuko and I watched the waves of the ocean and talked together about those things.

One day when I was alone, I asked myself, *Is she the one whom I have been dreaming about and waiting for?* And I knew the answer was yes. She was the one God had provided for me. I would not find a more ideal wife in the whole world. And I could not face the thought of a future without her.

We went again to the seashore, watching the gigantic Pacific Ocean and the waves splashing against the rocks. The day of my departure to S. M. U. was drawing close. We sat in the car and silently watched the waves for a while. She drew closer to me.

I told her honestly how difficult a minister's life was in Japan. He was always poor financially, and he had many worries for his church and for his church members. It would not be an easy life for the wife, especially an American-born girl.

And then I said to her, "You are the one I have been waiting and praying for. I believe you are God's answer to my prayer. I want you to marry me. I have been brought up in a very poor family and will continue to be poor for His sake. I have nothing to offer you except my love and the joy of serving Christ and his kingdom together. I believe that this can be a thrilling joy to both our hearts. There will be times when we must share suffering and hardship in the work of our ministry, yet the thankfulness of our hearts will be much greater than the hardships. I want you to marry me."

I knew that my proposal was not a surprise to her, because

we had the mutual feeling of being drawn closer and closer together by God.

She listened to me quietly and then answered in her sweet voice, "Yes, I will."

We were engaged that moment. I finally discovered my life's treasure in a strange land. No one arranged it. I asked no one to find a wife for me. Yet I believe profoundly that God arranged her for me and me for her.

I kissed her gently. Our kiss sealed our engagement sacredly and tightly. We certainly believed that Jesus Christ was with us when we became engaged.

We were quiet for a long time, holding hands tightly. In the quietness of our hearts we pledged loyalty to each other and to God and his kingdom.

Nobuko's parents were happy about our engagement. We set our wedding day for August 16, 1938, two years later, after my graduation from S. M. U.

"Nobuko," her father said, "Mr. Shimada is a poor student. I hope you are not expecting a diamond engagement ring from him. One who is dedicating her life to the ministry must not be so vain as to want a diamond ring."

"Yes, I understand, Father," she said. "I was not thinking about it."

A few days later Nobuko asked me for a Japanese Bible as a token of betrothal. That I could afford, and she was happy to receive it.

My own happiness was entire and complete.

15

Married at Last

What a beautiful city Santa Barbara was. I believe I would remember it that way even if it did not have the special significance for me of meeting my wife there.

The Japanese people were very friendly. Some of them I had met in Los Angeles before going to S. M. U., but even the strangers welcomed me like an old friend. They were really thirsty for the living water of the gospel. I preached every Sunday with faith, hope, and love. They seemed to appreciate my sermons, and their children learned the Japanese language rather quickly. I even taught them some of the Japanese songs.

One of my pupils in the Japanese language school was a quiet eleven-year-old boy named Leonard Honda. He learned Japanese well. He and I often played a game of Ping-Pong after class. His parents were not Christians, but they were sending their son to our Sunday school and language school.

One day this boy asked his father, "Dad, when Mr. Shimada goes back to school, will you please give him ten dollars as a present? He is a poor student from Japan."

Mr. Honda did not care to associate with others. His only interest seemed to be in his son and daughter and in making money for their education.

One day Leonard was playing with a rope on a tree in his backyard. He tied a hangman's knot and was accidently caught in the rope and choked to death. The father and mother were grief-stricken. He was their only son, and it seemed to them that the end of the world had come.

I officiated at the funeral service for this boy and often visited his home to comfort and strengthen the family. Mr. Honda was known as a man of strong will, but to me he was a man of tears and loneliness. He expressed his desire to learn more about Christianity, so I often talked with him about Christ and his kingdom.

Mr. Honda gradually changed. The gloomy expression on his face began to alter to one of radiance as he adjusted his attitude toward others. He became a generous and friendly man. He liked to attend church services. He liked to talk with people. He liked to visit those in trouble, offering help.

One day a family in Los Angeles lost a young son in an auto accident. Mr. Honda read about it in the Japanese newspapers. He sympathized with the parents, and he wrote a letter of comfort to them even though they were strangers to him. When he received a grateful reply from them and learned more of their suffering, he could not stay still. He took a day off from his work and went to visit them, ninety miles away, to share their sorrow.

When I was about ready to go back to school, he came to me and said, "My son once asked me to give ten dollars to Mr. Shimada as a present when he went back to school. I did not pay any attention then, but now I feel that it was my boy's prayer. So please let me help you in a small way. I will send you ten dollars every month. Please accept it."

I was deeply touched by his words. Ten dollars from his salary each month was not a small amount in those days. (He worked as a cook in a wealthy Caucasian home.) For two years, until I graduated from Southern Methodist University School of Theology, he sent me ten dollars faithfully each month, and each month I wrote him a letter and tried to lead him to the Christian faith. After I graduated from the seminary, his whole family came to the altar to be baptized by me.

In all my career in the ministry I have never come across anyone who changed so completely as this man did—from darkness to light; from a cold, gloomy individual to a warm, radiant personality; from a self-centered, unsociable person to a generous, saintly man. He passed away soon after the Second World War. He is another unforgettable person in my life.

Those three months in Santa Barbara passed like three days, and it was of course very hard to leave Nobuko.

When I left Santa Barbara that fall I had a little over $300. I had been able to save almost all the money I received as I was always invited by church members for meals and had almost no expenses. Thus when I returned to Southern Methodist, I had no financial worries for the second year.

Around the beginning of that year a stranger approached me, smiling, and introduced himself as a minister and graduate of the School of Theology of S. M. U. His name was William Justice. He asked me to come to his church and give my testimony, which I did the next Sunday. His daughter, a cute little girl about five or six years old, reminded me of Shirley Temple.

In the Reverend Justice's church I talked about my conversion and how I decided to become a minister. Mr. Justice was pleased with my testimony and insisted that I bring it to many Caucasian churches. He opened the way for me. I received invitations that year from many churches in Texas. Practically every weekend I visited some church, and every time I shared my testimony with a church I received a gratuity. Thus during the second year I saved enough money for my third and last year at S. M. U.

I have appreciated the kindness of Mr. Justice throughout my life. When my son was born in San Francisco in 1948, I named him Justin after my good friend, the Reverend Justice.

When the second summer vacation came, I decided not to work for money but to study for my graduation thesis. I spent the whole three months in a little cottage on a hill near Santa Barbara. The cottage belonged to Mr. and Mrs. Nishida. Mr. Nishida, a member of the official board of the Japanese church in Santa Barbara, was the one who first wrote to me, inviting me to serve his church as a summer minister. This kind couple treated me like their own son, and I regarded them as my parents in America.

The topic of my thesis was "Christology of the Fourth Gospel." I read fifteen good books about the Gospel of John and collected a great deal of material. I read the fourth Gospel in Greek twice during the vacation. I almost memorized the whole Gospel of John in Japanese.

When I returned to school, I was nearly ready to send my thesis to the typist and did not need to be bothered by it during the final year in the seminary. It was fortunate that I had my thesis complete, for in the third year I was busy again giving testimony in churches throughout Texas.

I graduated from Southern Methodist University School of Theology in 1938, receiving a Bachelor of Divinity degree (now called Master of Theology). My scholastic standing was about average. I did well in some courses and poor in others. After all, I was a foreign student; I should not expect too much. I was satisfied with my record. During the last chapel hour Dean Hawk gave me an opportunity to speak for a few minutes about my experiences in the school.

I stood up and said, "I do not feel that I have spent three years in this school. It seems like three months. I have been extremely happy here. I am sorry my knowledge of English was not adequate and that I gave bad times to all the professors because of this language handicap. Here I apologize to all the professors from the bottom of my heart. You know, during my first year in this school I felt as though I were reading a book in the darkness; in the second year I felt as if I were reading in the moonlight; in the third year I began to read at dawn.

"I am glad that I have met many fine students who are going to the vineyard of God's kingdom. I am sure that some of them will become outstanding leaders in the spiritual world. Wherever I may go I will always remember this school as my alma mater."

The audience applauded me warmly. I was finally graduated from Southern Methodist University School of Theology. To my surprise I had $200 in the bank, the same amount I had when I first landed in America.

God had indeed helped me.

When I returned to Santa Barbara for our wedding, I found that Nobuko had been working too hard, mostly in church activities. She was close to a nervous breakdown. She was in bed all the time, she was weak, she had lost her appetite, and she was losing weight. Her doctor said that the only thing wrong with her was fatigue. She had been doing three times more than her small body could do. The poor girl was so ambitious and conscientious, but she did not have the robust physique to cope with all she wanted to do.

The wedding day was approaching, but she did not show any signs of improvement. Her mother thought it was something more serious than fatigue.

"Shigeo-san," she said, "my daughter has been in bed for almost forty days, and there is no sign of her getting better. Would you like to postpone the wedding?"

"No," I said, "I want to marry her on the scheduled day. If she cannot get up, we will have our wedding ceremony in her bedroom. If she has to go to heaven, she will go as Mrs. Shimada, not Miss Imai."

Mrs. Imai was happy, and she told Nobuko. Strangely, from that day Nobuko started to eat well, and just two days before the wedding day she got up and was strong enough to get ready for a small home wedding.

To me it was almost a miracle. We had a very simple wedding ceremony in her home with just the family and a few close friends present.

She had long dreamed of wearing a white wedding gown at her wedding. I suggested that she be practical and wear an ordinary dress. It was all right with me, and I thought a wedding gown was an extravagance. Nobuko agreed with me.

As she needed to rest more, I took her to a quiet camping grounds in the mountain behind the city. We spent our honeymoon there, close to God and nature.

I took good care of her for a week. Quietness, fresh air and sunshine made her better and better. However, she was not strong enough to go to Boston with me as we had originally planned, so I had to leave her with her parents while I went to Boston University alone.

For a long time I considered our wedding ceremony perfect. Then while we were in charge of the Alameda Methodist Church in 1940 and 1941, a young couple celebrated their first wedding anniversary. My wife and I were invited to their home. During the evening, while the men were chatting, the hostess and other women guests went into another room and just for fun put the hostess's wedding gown on my wife and brought her in front of me. I was surprised at the sight and was speechless for a while. I beheld my bride in a wedding gown for the first time.

"I really wanted to wear this kind of white wedding gown on our wedding day," she said.

I remembered that she had mentioned it at the time of our wedding, and I had discouraged her. Now I deeply regretted my thoughtlessness, and felt sorry for her. Now she did not have a memory of a bridal veil.

I have often scolded myself for that.

16

On to Boston University

I chose Boston University School of Theology for study toward my degree of Master of Sacred Theology because I had been deeply impressed by Dr. Knudson of the Boston faculty when he came to S. M. U. for a series of special lectures. Going to Boston was a big step for me and a financially difficult one. I had only $200 to start the year and no definite prospects for earning more money. My wife had savings of her own from giving piano lessons and wanted to help me, but I told her that I was sure I could take care of myself under any circumstances. There were times during the next year when I was to doubt that.

When I arrived at the school in Boston, I was surprised to see a very old building. It did not look like a college but more like a big, old apartment house. However, that old building had everything in it. It had the dormitory, a big library, a large chapel, all the necessary classrooms, and even a big gym. The one disadvantage was that it had no dining room, and all the students had to eat somewhere else. Now Boston University School of Theology has beautiful new buildings.

On the first day I met Dr. Knudson personally. He was my major professor. He gave me some instructions about his course. He looked like a prophet to me rather than a theologian.

I met Dr. Brightman, who was my minor professor. He seemed very intellectual. He also gave me instructions about his course. However, he spoke so fast that I could not follow him at that time. Later I understood his lectures well.

I also met Dean Marlatt. He was a poet and theologian, a man of warm heart. He kindly gave me a scholarship that covered tuition and room but not meals.

My $200 was gone in three months. I did not tell my wife this as I had been so positive I could take care of myself that I wanted to show her I could.

I got a job washing dishes in a Swedish smorgasbord restaurant for two hours a day. Later I worked four hours a day. I understood that the immigration law now permitted foreign students to work, and several foreign students I knew had dishwashing jobs. I was fast at washing dishes even though it was my first experience. (They did not have electric dishwashers in those days.) I thought I was almost an expert. The boss of the restaurant seemed satisfied with my work. (My wife does not believe this story as even today I am rather slow when I help her in the kitchen.)

Working two hours a day was not so bad, but working four hours after school was hard. Every night around 10:30 P.M. I came back to the dormitory almost worn out.

One night after a hard four hours of work at the sink I left the restaurant. One of the waitresses, a very pretty girl, who had gone out the door just before me, stopped and stretched out her hand.

"Come on," she said. "I'll walk to your dormitory with you."

I was surprised, for such an action was unknown to me in my world in Japan. It was not that I thought there was anything wrong about her intentions; she meant to be friendly and wanted to walk home with me to keep me company. She probably thought I was lonesome. I just could not picture a young lady, who according to my training should have been shy and passive, making such an aggressive suggestion.

"What are you waiting for?" she said. "Give me your hand."

I thought, *This is America. Do as the Americans do.*

I tried to reach out my hand to her, but it would not move an inch. I felt as if my arm were tied to me with an iron chain. I was not thinking of my wife in California because I was not intending to do anything wrong. I was not thinking much of anything. I just could not move my hand.

"What's the matter?" she asked. "Are you afraid of a girl?"

She walked away from me while I stood there feeling my right arm to see if it were paralyzed. I tried to raise it, and this time I had no trouble. A psychologist could probably explain it in scientific terms, but I just felt paralyzed.

Years later I told my wife of the incident. She was amused and said, "That was just like you."

I continued working until summer vacation came. I was often tempted to write to my wife to ask for money, but I did not. My father taught me when I was a small boy: "A Japanese man should not be supported financially by a woman." I followed his teaching in this case.

Spending four hours in the restaurant every evening meant a great sacrifice as far as school work was concerned. I was always behind schedule. I needed thirty hours a day; twenty-four was not enough.

I wanted to visit the many historic places in Boston and its vicinity on weekends, but I had to work hard to catch up with my studies. Accordingly, I saw very few historic places even though I was in Boston nearly a year.

When summer vacation came I hurried back to Santa Barbara to be with my wife. Her health was much better than I expected. She thought that she was strong enough to go with me to Boston the second year, which made life seem much brighter.

The annual conference of the Pacific Japanese Methodist Mission was in session in San Francisco. I thought it was a good idea to pay my respects to all the Japanese ministers there; so on the last day of the session I visited the conference. I was introduced to the members of the conference and was given a chance to say a few words.

I do not remember what I said in this talk. Later Dr. Frank Herron Smith, the superintendent of the conference, came to me and asked me to help two small rural churches as a student pastor. He said that it would fill a great need. Because it was the last day of the conference and the Bishop's appointments would be read within a few hours, he could give me only one hour to decide.

I went to a quiet room and meditated for an hour and then

decided to accept the position. Dr. Smith was pleased with my decision. He advised me to transfer from Boston University School of Theology to Pacific School of Religion in Berkeley and continue my study there. I followed his advice.

I enrolled in the Pacific School of Religion and studied under Dr. John C. Bennett. An arrangement was made with Boston University to have three credits sent there from Pacific toward my Master of Sacred Theology degree. Thus I received this degree from Boston University in 1940.

I was appointed to two small churches in the Sacramento Valley. A sixty-year-old parsonage on Sixth Street in Oakland was given to us. It was a dilapidated, flea-infested house but our first real home.

The following year we moved to Alameda where I was appointed to a church. I continued graduate studies at Pacific School of Religion at the same time.

And then the war came to tear us from this happy, peaceful existence.

17

Waves of Pearl Harbor

During World War II I was still a Japanese citizen, but I was living in the United States and felt bound by duty to obey its laws and uphold its interests. I never encouraged the young nisei to become conscientious objectors. When one of my church members joined the army, I encouraged him and prayed for him. When one became a conscientious objector, and acted accordingly, I also encouraged and prayed for him. I do not believe that this makes me an opportunist. I simply respect and admire any person who has sincere convictions and acts accordingly.

December 7, 1941, started for us as for all others as just another peaceful Sunday. I was continuing my graduate studies in the Pacific School of Religion and was a student minister of the Alameda Japanese Methodist Church. We held morning services as usual. After the service I returned to the parsonage and casually turned on the radio. I thought my ears were deceiving me when I heard the announcer blast out the almost unbelievable words: "Surprise Jap attack on Pearl Harbor!"

My first feeling was of deep sorrow. I was convinced that this attack was the beginning of Japan's downfall. The Japanese militarists had gone too far and were destroying themselves and their nation. Their aims and their actions were not acceptable in the sight of God. All of the Japanese people would suffer extreme hardship because of this war.

The next few months were an anxious time for us. It was a period of hysteria; people believed that the Japanese on the

West Coast were waiting for an opportunity to sabotage vital installations, that an invasion was coming. There were actual physical threats. One midnight a voice in front of our house shouted, "Japs, come out! I will shoot you all!" I did not really think whoever it was meant to kill us, but it was not a good feeling.

It was, then, in some sense to me a relief when in May of 1942, all the Japanese living in Alameda, Oakland, and San Francisco were ordered to enter the Tanforan Assembly Center. The barbed wire, the guards in the watch towers, meant that we could not get out, but they also meant that no outsider could get in to harm us. Some did not look on it as a concentration camp but as a protection from the violent and angry people outside, although it was not the intent of the government to protect us.

To most of the *issei* (Japanese-born) people who came to America from Japan and who could not be naturalized under existing law such an order was not altogether a surprise. They recognized that they were technically enemy aliens even though they might have been in America for many years. However, the American-born nisei were extremely shocked; they were American citizens.

Before the evacuation we held our final service in our church. I told the congregation, "You and I are and will be suffering a great deal because of this war. This is an opportunity to test our Christian faith. Let us meet all suffering face to face and endure the coming tribulations patiently. Let us not give up hope, whatever our trial may be. I assure you that a new, better world will be born through our suffering just as a new life is born through the sacrifice and suffering of a mother who gives birth to a child. Remember, you are all Christians and you are all citizens of the kingdom of God. The issei people are called enemy aliens, and unfortunately the nisei are treated like aliens as well. However, we must not become enemy aliens of God. Please behave as children of God wherever you may go and whatever your situation may be."

The evacuees were transported in special Greyhound buses to the assembly center, a first step before being sent to an internment camp. An army guard stood beside the driver at attention with a bayonet, facing the evacuees. Everyone was gravely quiet; there was not a sound, not even from the small children aboard.

The Tanforan Assembly Center, ten miles south of San Francisco, was a race track. There were many stables and one big building. Single men were placed in the big building, but most of us were housed in stables. Some of the stables were new and clean, but most were very shabby.

My wife, my mother-in-law, and I were assigned to one of the worst stables. There was a pile of fresh manure outside the door. The stall had been whitewashed inside without being cleaned first, and the floor was covered with a cheap linoleum. A strong odor of manure filled the air. When I lifted the linoleum, we discovered raw manure all over the floor. We had no broom nor anything to clean the floor with; so we just covered it with the linoleum as it was.

Day and night we lived uncomfortably with the smell of manure. Soon our clothes and even our bodies began to smell of this disagreeable odor. I felt resentment about being treated like an animal. I could understand the bitter feeling of Americans toward the Japanese militarists who treacherously attacked Pearl Harbor. I myself was angry about the attack. But the Japanese people in America had nothing to do with it.

As I fretted over this unfortunate circumstance, my thoughts turned to Jesus Christ who was born in a stable that must have been much worse than ours. It was not whitewashed. The floor was not covered with linoleum. It must have been filthy with the manure of animals. According to the Gospel of Luke, baby Jesus was wrapped with cloths and was placed in the manger. It was fortunate that Mary had cloths; otherwise baby Jesus would have been wrapped with straw just like a baby animal. Yet Mary and Joseph did not complain about their miserable situation. When the shepherds came to meet Jesus and worship him, it was a heavenly picture. I am sure that the stable was full of glory.

However, in another stable of the twentieth century there was nothing but the spirit of resentment and bitterness. Why such a difference between the two stables? It was a difference of the hearts. Mary, Joseph, and the shepherds were profoundly related with God, whereas God was absent in my heart in our stable. I was deeply ashamed of myself. When I realized that being put in a stable as the holy family had been was a unique experience, a spirit of peace replaced the resentment and bitterness in my heart.

We were in Tanforan for five months, and the worst row of stalls, which included ours, was condemned by the San Mateo County Health Department about two weeks after our arrival. We were moved into small new barracks that were built in the center of the race track. At the end of September, we were all moved to the War Relocation Center in Topaz, Utah. We lived there in drab black barracks in the heart of the desert.

When we discuss this evacuation of the Japanese, citizens and noncitizens alike, we must remember that it is not fair to judge an action taken during the hysteria of war with the same severity we would judge the same action taken in a calm and peaceful atmosphere. War came suddenly to the American people; they were not ready for war. The people and the government were in a state of confusion. There was the genuine fear that the West Coast would be invaded. "They are all Japs and not to be trusted" was the feeling. There was a need for people to see that the government was taking some positive action. However, when I look at what the government did to the Japanese-Americans from the present calm detachment, I would say that it was a grave mistake.

The nisei were American citizens. They were taught in school that their American citizenship was a thing to be treasured. They did treasure it and were proud of that citizenship. Yet they were treated as enemy aliens and put into a barbed wire camp without trial or excuse other than their ancestry. Historically, it was a mistake. The Japanese-Americans and their issei parents were law-abiding, honest, hard-working people. The evacuation caused many of them to lose all that they had. The extent of loss that some of the successful Japanese-Americans suffered was so great that they could never be repaid. To many the traumatic experience had a lasting psychological and emotional effect.

The living conditions in Topaz were better than we expected. There was plenty of hot water for the shower rooms and the laundry rooms and enough coal for fuel. We had a grade school and a high school in the center, with both Caucasian and Japanese-American teachers. The children of the administration officers attended these schools with the children of the evacuees.

We had ample food in the center; babies and children had enough milk although this was in short supply on the outside. At one time I heard that people on the outside stopped a train carrying food to the center saying they wanted milk for their children. They thought it was not fair that the Japanese in the center had enough milk while they went without. The man in charge of the train said that as long as he lived he would obey the government order; the food would not be taken from him. It is my understanding that the food in the center was the same ration as was given to the army because we were under the jurisdiction of the army.

It is my belief that the government did the best that it could under the circumstances. Many Japanese felt that the evacuation order was requested by Caucasian farmers and businessmen who wanted to profit by the evacuation. Such requests may have been made for that reason, but I do not believe that they influenced the action of the government.

There were about 8,000 Japanese people of all ages in the Topaz center. It was rather a peaceful life at first. Some of the administration officers were very fine Christians who worshiped with the evacuee congregation on Sundays. The assistant project director and his wife, Mr. and Mrs. Roscoe E. Bell, were particularly concerned about the welfare of the evacuees, and they showed kindness in many ways. Mrs. Bell, an accomplished musician, served as the director of the choir in our United Protestant church and led an eighty-voice Christmas choir in the "Hallelujah Chorus" from Handel's *Messiah.*

I do not know about the other centers, but before long the peace in our desert camp of Topaz came to an end. Japanese agitators began to rise here and there. They tried to lead the American-born Japanese to anti-Americanism. Their argument was: "If America regards you as her citizens, why are you in this barbed-wire camp? America does not want your loyalty. You are after all Japanese, and your loyalty must be to Japan."

I do not believe that these agitators were organized or paid by the Japanese government. Their methods were too childish and beyond common sense. They nevertheless managed to cause a great deal of trouble. The center was under the authority of the administration office, where a handful of Caucasians worked, but it was actually a little Japan. For a time the agitators dominated the entire center.

Many of the rumors they spread would seem beyond belief, and yet some simple people believed them. The Christian ministers were called spies; they were accused of being paid by the American government to make the people pro-American. The agitators invented war news and repeated it throughout the center, claiming to have heard it on a special secret broadcast from Japan. Every day they reported several American battleships, cruisers, and carriers destroyed. The American Navy was sunk several times over by those imaginary broadcasts.

The agitators reported that Japanese soldiers were about to invade the West Coast and liberate all Japanese from the centers. Those who stood bravely against American propaganda and were faithful to Japan would be appointed governors of California, Oregon, and Washington and mayors of Los Angeles, San Francisco, Portland, and Seattle. Nothing was too ridiculous for some to believe. There was the story that the Emperor of Japan sent his personally written greetings to the Japanese in the center through the Spanish ambassador but that a Christian minister destroyed it.

I do not know the number of the agitators, but it was not large. The percentages varied according to the groups to which they belonged. There were the issei, who were born in Japan. There were the nisei, born in America and raised in America. (There were no nisei among the agitators.) There were also the kibei, born in America but sent to Japan in early childhood to be educated and who then returned to America as young people. Not all the *kibei* were pro-Japan, but quite a few were. They were agitators themselves or followed the agitators and made lots of trouble in the center.

The issei, born in Japan and restricted by law from becoming citizens of the United States, were naturally more sympathetic to Japan. They had always been law-abiding residents of

America, however, and I think they would have continued to be and would have caused no trouble at all if they had not been displaced by the evacuation. The agitators would have had no chance to excite them; they would have heard the true news of the war, and they would have been busy working, sharing the war prosperity and adding to the manpower of America.

The nisei were, of course, in a miserable situation. When war broke out, they expected and wanted to fight against Germany and Japan along with the rest of the American citizens. Instead, they were put into the center.

There was a strong feeling of bitterness among them for a time, which the agitators tried to use, but they were generally unsuccessful. The nisei could not become pro-Japanese because they did not know Japan. Everything about it was alien to them. It was natural for them to be bitter—anyone is in danger of becoming bitter if he or she feels he or she has been treated unjustly. Bitterness and anti-Americanism, however, were two different things. The nisei were generally loyal to America. It was no surprise to me that once they had the opportunity to prove their loyalty, the 442nd Regimental Combat Team (all nisei) became the most decorated regiment in the United States Army.

However, even among the nisei there were exceptions. Some nisei were persuaded by their parents to give up their American citizenship and become Japanese citizens. Most of them did not know what this really meant to them. Their numbers were small, but they had a strong propaganda value for the agitators. The agitators used them by saying, "Even the American-born Japanese have the Japanese spirit."

Those who gave up their citizenship were sent to Japan on exchange ships. In general they could not adjust themselves to Japan. They had an unhappy time there, and after the war most of them tried to regain their American citizenship. Nothing speaks more strongly for the broad-minded generosity of America than the fact that in most cases their citizenship was restored, and they were allowed to return to the United States.

The agitators knew that the Reverend Taro Goto and I were strongly against this anti-American movement. This enraged the agitators, who were said to have made up a black list of people to be eliminated. The Reverend Mr. Goto was supposed to be the first name on this list, my own name the second, and the other ministers the third and fourth names.

One night Mr. Goto was attacked and almost killed by a masked man who struck at him with a lead pipe as he left the shower room. Mr. Goto escaped to his barracks, but as he opened the door the man leaped at him again from behind and shattered the door with a blow that missed its target.

The bishop of the Methodist Church appointed Mr. Goto to the Japanese church in Denver, Colorado, to protect him from further attacks. This promoted me to the top of the list. It was not a promotion I especially enjoyed.

I became a cautious man as far as my movements were concerned, though I did not change my thinking or my attitude. I did not go out at night except to church meetings, and my barracks was guarded by a faithful church member who was a member of the evacuee police force. I was never actually attacked.

18
A Nisei Soldier

In the spring of 1944, an army officer visited the Topaz center to recruit American-born Japanese for the United States Army. He emphasized repeatedly that this was a good opportunity for nisei to show their capability as well as to prove their loyalty.

The agitators in the center made good use of this in their propaganda. They said, "Now America is losing the war and is short of soldiers. America is now asking nisei to volunteer. What a laugh! Remember, America put you into the internment camp, and now the government is asking you to show your loyalty. What a contradiction!"

In spite of such talk about 100 sincere young boys volunteered from our camp. Nobuo Kajiwara was one of them.

When Nobuo asked his parents to allow him to volunteer, they pleaded with him to wait until he was drafted. As he was an only son, it was quite natural for them to feel this way. However, Nobuo's determination was so strong that they were unable to change his mind.

Realizing their inability to keep their son from volunteering, Mr. and Mrs. Kajiwara came to me for help. I personally believed that it was not a good idea to prevent his volunteering; on the other hand, I fully understood their feelings as parents.

"I cannot promise you that I will stop your son," I said, "but give me a chance for a heart-to-heart talk with him. If he wants to volunteer just to exchange this monotonous camp life for a wild life in the outside world, then I will stop him, but if it is from a pure spirit of self-sacrifice and patriotism, I cannot interfere."

They understood my point. Late that night Nobuo came to my barracks. "Reverend Shimada," he said, "my parents asked me to come to you. I have come, but not because I want to hear your opinion about volunteering. I have made up my mind already. No one can stop me. I came to you because I want to tell you what is in my heart, and I want you to help my parents understand. I can't bear to see them so sad."

When he said this, his eyes were full of tears, and his hands were trembling. For a few minutes I could not say even a word. I finally broke the silence by asking him four questions.

First I said, "As a son it is your duty to be obedient to your parents. Now they are asking you not to volunteer, but you are going to do so, rejecting their plea. Don't you feel sorry for them?"

"Yes," he said, "I am very unhappy and sad when I consider my parents' feelings. I have heard that many parents in America, as well as in Japan, are encouraging their sons to volunteer. But we Americans of Japanese ancestry are in a very difficult situation. Our parents are subjects of Japan, ineligible to become naturalized citizens, and we their sons are Americans whose loyalty is to America.

"Our parents are put in a great dilemma. My heart bleeds for them. After a hard struggle I decided to volunteer. I know my parents will suffer a great deal, but I feel I must be loyal to America. I know that someday they will appreciate what I have done."

The second question I asked was this: "Can't you wait until you are drafted? Your parents are not asking you to go against your nation at all. They merely want you to wait. I am quite sure that they will want you to do your best for your country when you are drafted. If you wait until then, you can satisfy your parents and also serve your country. Why can't you wait?"

"I had been thinking that way too," he said, "but several friends of mine have volunteered recently. I talked with them, and I came to realize that all of them are going from a spirit of self-sacrifice, not selfishness. They made me feel ashamed of myself. It seems to me that it is not good to wait until I'm drafted; it would be cowardly. I've never sacrificed myself for any noble cause; I'm disgusted with myself. Now this is a chance for me to be born again as a man. To me there is a great difference between volunteering and being drafted. So I can't wait. I'll volunteer."

I asked the third question: "You are American-born, so you have American citizenship; yet you have been put into this barbed-wire camp, and your freedom as a citizen has been denied in the center. In other words, you have not been treated as an American by your government. Do you still want to volunteer for America?"

"When I was forced to enter the assembly center," he said, "I felt as though I was being persecuted by my own government. I was so angry with the government that I wanted to give up my citizenship and become a Japanese subject. I actually looked at the map of Japan, but I simply couldn't feel that it was my country. I saw the flag of Japan, but I didn't feel any enthusiasm for it. On the contrary, when I saw the stars and stripes, my heart burned with patriotism even in this relocation center. I realized that after all I am an American, and I came to the conclusion that I must not be bothered by a little thing like this evacuation.

"I have been benefited by this country more than words can express. I am a loyal American even though my government is not just to me. I will volunteer not for the government but for the beautiful and ideal America that I hold in my heart."

I asked my last question rather emphatically, "Then you are determined to die for America, are you?"

"Just a minute, Reverend," he said. "Volunteering doesn't mean I'm going to join the suicide squad. My point is not to die but to dedicate myself toward our victory. To tell the truth, I really want to come back alive after we win the war. However, if it is necessary for me to die on the battle front, I think I am ready."

"Forgive me for asking you such questions," I said. "I feel as if I have been talking with a great preacher. Your attitude and your ideas are sincere and noble. Everybody who knows your spirit toward your country will respect you. I am a minister, but you have just taught me a great spiritual lesson. I promise you that I will tell your parents about your strong and noble determination and will try to change their attitude."

Early the next morning, while I was still in bed, Mr. and Mrs. Kajiwara called at my barracks. Anxiously they searched my eyes, wondering what my reply would be. I told them the details of my conversation with Nobuo, and I asked them to give him their blessing.

After a deep and long sigh, the father said, "We now understand him very well. We have been wrong. After all, he is an American. It is his duty and privilege to sacrifice himself for his country. We will encourage him."

Nobuo then volunteered for the United States Army. When his final training was nearing completion and he was about to be sent overseas, his parents asked me to write a letter to strengthen his spirit. I wrote:

> Dear Nobuo:
>
> You have dedicated yourself to your country. It is a beautiful thing. I am proud of you. Remember, your body and heart are not yours anymore because they have been dedicated to your country. If you spoil your body and heart in some unclean place, it is against the spirit of volunteering; it is throwing yourself away rather than dedicating.
>
> I am sure through your own dedication you can understand the great meaning of the sacrifice of Jesus Christ on the cross. He dedicated himself to the kingdom of God just as you have dedicated yourself to the beautiful America that you hold in your heart. Jesus Christ fought a good fight, and when the time came, he sacrificed himself on his battle front, the cross.
>
> I want you to fight bravely for your nation and for humanity, and it if is necessary, sacrifice yourself for your nation just as Jesus Christ did on the cross for the kingdom of God.
>
> Your friend in Christ,
> Shigeo Shimada

I handed the letter to my wife to type. After she read it she said, "Do you really mean to send such a cold letter to Nobuo, who is about to go to the battle front? Can't you write a warmer and more comforting letter to him?"

"No," I said, "I know what I am writing. I understand the spirit of volunteering. I myself volunteered to serve in the kingdom of God. When one volunteer writes a letter to another, his letter should be like this. Please type it as it is and do not change even a word."

Later, I heard from Mr. and Mrs. Kajiwara that when Nobuo read my letter in the army camp, he wept over it and shared it with many Japanese-American volunteers in his regiment.

I received one letter from Nobuo. It read in part: "Here I am in Italy now. Thank you for your kind encouragement. I think I can face the future with conviction and quite a bit of courage."

A few weeks later he was killed in action.

The report of Nobuo's death brought me deep sorrow, and the beautiful and profound impression he left with me was permanently carved on my heart.

I found myself walking to a quiet spot in the desert camp and speaking to him: "Nobuo, I respect you. It is written in the Bible, 'Unless a grain of wheat falls into the earth and dies, it remains alone; but if it dies, it bears much fruit.' I am sure your death will bring much fruit in the land of America which is your beloved and only nation and to which you sacrificed your young life. Be in peace in the heavenly kingdom."

All these years later, I still remember every word Nobuo spoke to me. He was the only son of Mr. and Mrs. Kajiwara. Once Mrs. Kajiwara said to me, "Reverend Shimada, whenever I meet you, you remind me of my son, and somehow I am comforted deeply when I am with you."

Even today, deeply though I regret Nobuo's death, I do not feel that I did the wrong thing in not trying to discourage him from volunteering. I had a strong feeling that he would be killed, but it seemed to me that he had the right to choose as he did.

I still believe that his death on the battlefield was not an accident. He chose his way bravely and went his way and finished his way. Because of that his death was meaningful to himself and to the nation. In the bottom of his heart he hoped to come back alive, but that does not indicate contradiction or confusion. He recognized the possibility of dying when he dedicated himself to the nation.

I have told his story because I think he fairly reflects the spirit of the average young nisei of his day.

19

"Correction, Please"

For my wife and me life in the camp in the desert of Utah brought a happiness and blessing that was far more important than our problems. Our daughter Gloria Kumiko was born there.

We had been married for six years, and had almost given up hope of having children. Then one day my wife came back from visiting the doctor at the center and gave me the wonderful news. We were going to be parents!

The baby was born on September 2, 1944, in the center hospital. It was Saturday, about 9 A.M., and I was preparing a sermon in the church office when a church member came to me and said "It's a boy!"

This man spread the news all over the center. On the way to the hospital to see my wife and son I stopped by the post office and sent a wire to my brother-in-law in Boulder, Colorado: "It's a boy!" Yuji was teaching Japanese at the Naval Language School there.

As I left the post office, I met a woman who had been a member of my church in Alameda. "Congratulations," she said. "Your daughter is cute."

"You mean my son," I said.

"No," she said, "your daughter is cute."

It was all very confusing. Now "he" was a "she."

"How did my son become a daughter?" I asked.

"You had better go to the hospital and see for yourself," she said.

134

I hurried to the hospital where I visited my wife first.

"We have a little girl, five pounds nine ounces," she said, smiling at me.

"Thank you for a cute girl."

"Don't thank me, thank God," was her answer.

I went to the baby quarters and met my daughter. The news was right about one thing; she was cute. "I have been waiting for you for six years," I told her. "I'm glad you finally arrived safely."

On the way home I sent another wire to my brother-in-law. "My baby boy is a girl."

The next day I was scheduled to preach to the Japanese-speaking congregation. By that time everyone knew that I had become a father and that my baby was a boy for a while and then turned out to be a girl.

The liturgist announced, "Yesterday morning a baby girl was born to the Reverend and Mrs. Shimada. Mr. Shimada was so happy he shouted 'Oh boy!' Naturally everyone who heard him thought it was a boy and spread the news around the center."

My daughter quickly became the center of our family. My mother-in-law was busy washing for her, my wife was busy feeding her, and I was busy watching her. Somehow all of us were occupied or at least we felt we were busy. Our family life became more meaningful and much brighter. She was a healthy baby even though my wife was not a strong woman at that time.

I wanted to name her Gloria because of the religious significance. My wife gave her the Japanese middle name "Kumiko," meaning "child of eternal beauty."

I have been asked whether I was disappointed that the baby was a girl. To tell the truth, I was perhaps a little disappointed for a moment, as at the time we thought it was our first and last chance for a baby. We had no idea that four years later we would be blessed with a boy. The Japanese traditionally hope for a son to carry on the family name.

But our daughter brought so much joy into our lives that there was really no time to feel disappointment. Gloria continues to be our pride and joy. When she was graduating from

Lewis and Clark High School in Spokane as valedictorian, she made a decision to become a teacher of blind children. She felt that this was God's calling, just as God had called her father to ministry. Today she is a dedicated teacher in this field.

Today I am profoundly grateful to God for his blessings upon us for we have both a daughter and a son. There is a popular saying in Japan: "First girl, second boy." According to that interpretation of an ideal situation, our order was perfect.

20

A Little White Lie

E arly in 1945, the War Relocation Authority helped the evacuees to relocate from the Topaz center to the East and Midwest. Many moved to Chicago. We understood that the San Francisco Bay area was not yet open to Japanese because the tension there was still acute. Many were anxious to return to their homes, and a rumor started that some Japanese had gone back to San Francisco. Letters were actually received from those who had returned.

I went to the administration office to see just what the situation was and found that the answer was "yes" and "no."

"The San Francisco Bay Area has recently been opened to Japanese by the government," the director told me. "As you know, it is still a very critical spot. We are afraid that something unpleasant may happen if the Japanese return in a conspicuous group so we aren't encouraging it. However, we have permitted a few people to go back there more or less as test cases. These Japanese cannot live in their own houses yet, nor can they get a job. They are living together in a church building in Oakland and are waiting for the day when the tension eases. That is the way it stands now."

Although I could easily imagine the difficulties around San Francisco, I asked the director to let me go there to see the general situation for myself. He agreed and gave me a special letter to be used in the event of trouble.

Around the latter part of March, 1945, I went to Oakland. Seven Japanese were living quietly together in the education building of the old Oakland Japanese Methodist Church at West and Tenth Streets. I joined them. They told me that so far no Japanese were in San Francisco and that they were afraid to go to the city.

"I will go to San Francisco tomorrow to see the situation," I said.

They warned me to be very cautious and to avoid trouble because after all I was still an enemy alien. The next day I took the Key System, a train running between Oakland and San Francisco.

On the train I held a newspaper, not to read but more or less to hide myself behind. I saw a Japanese at the other end of the train. When I gave him a friendly nod, he responded with a warm smile. Then he started to come toward me. I thought that it would be conspicuous if two Japanese sat down together and talked in Japanese. I wanted to stop him from coming, but there was no way to do so.

He came to me smiling and sat down beside me. I hesitated to speak in Japanese, and while I was wondering whether I should use English or Japanese, he began to talk to me—in Chinese!

"Oh, oh," I said to myself, "he's Chinese. I should be careful. I should avoid any trouble."

The Chinese gentleman finished his talk and awaited my reply. I had no idea what he said. The situation was a little bit delicate.

"I'm sorry, I don't speak Chinese," I said.

"Oh, I see." He spoke good English. "What is your nationality?"

I knew that a Christian should not tell a lie, but I did not wish to create any trouble on the train. I thought a little white lie would be permissible in this case.

"I am a Korean," I answered in a small voice. I wanted to drop the conversation at that point, but to this Chinese it was just the beginning.

He smiled and said, "You know, Chinese and Koreans should be brothers from now on. After all, you and I belong to the same race. By the way, what is your name?"

This mess was getting worse and worse. That is the way it

goes even with white lies. I had to think up a Korean name quickly. I recalled a Korean classmate from Southern Methodist.

"My name is Park," I said. "You know, P-A-R-K, like a national park."

"That's an easy name to remember." He seemed pleased with my new Korean name. "Are you married?"

"No, I am not married."

My answer came out so quickly I didn't have time to think about it. It was certainly a lie and one my wife would not like very well either. There wasn't even much sense to it except that in my confused state I felt that if I said I was married he would ask about my wife and about my children and all sorts of things. I wanted this conversation to end as soon as possible.

"How old are you?" he asked.

"I am thirty-one years old," I said.

As I was thirty-eight at the time, this was becoming ridiculous. My reasoning, insofar as I was reasoning at all, was that I had already told him I was single and I felt guilty about it. I felt that I had repudiated my faithful wife. I knew I looked younger than my actual age. I chose "thirty-one" because I had been single then. It made me feel a little better about saying I was single.

"You're young," he said. "You're kinda nice looking. Shall I find a pretty young Korean girl for you?"

This was going much too far; I began to be very disturbed.

"Oh, no, no," I said. "I want to be single for a while."

"Okay, okay, don't be excited. I'm single too, and I'm enjoying the bachelor life," he said. "By the way, there is a good Korean restaurant in San Francisco. I'll take you there, and we can talk some more."

"I'm sorry, but I'm very busy today. Thank you just the same," I said. I knew my face was flushed.

"By the way, where are you living now?" he asked.

This kindly Chinese gentleman was certainly the most inquisitive person I had ever met. I could not tell him I was living in the Oakland Japanese Methodist Church; so I told him I lived in San Francisco.

"Fine, fine. I have my office in San Francisco. I know the city from corner to corner. In what part of San Francisco are you living?" It seemed that his questions would never stop.

I knew that the San Francisco Japanese Methodist Church was located on Pine Street. "Pine Street," I said.

"What number?"

"I forgot the number, but it is near Bush Street."

"But, Mr. Park, every spot on Pine Street is near Bush Street, because Pine and Bush are parallel."

What a miserable situation. I was not even a good liar.

"Well, sir," I said, "I am a newcomer. I just arrived here a few days ago." This was the only true statement I had made during the conversation.

"Now I understand. I thought something was funny from the beginning."

I felt extremely uncomfortable when he said that.

"What are you going to do in San Francisco? If there is any way I can help you, I will be glad to do so. After all, Chinese and Koreans are brothers." His tone was friendly.

"Thank you very much for your kindness. I may need your help and advice someday but not right now. I am just observing the general situation in San Francisco," I answered.

The train reached San Francisco, and we got off. "Mr. Park," my Chinese friend said, "I am a Christian, a member of the Presbyterian church. I like to help people in trouble. Here is my card. If you ever need my help, just give me a ring. Remember, Chinese and Koreans are brothers." And he went his way.

I felt relieved and ashamed. I merely wanted to avoid trouble, but what a mess I had made! Practically all my answers were lies, unnecessary lies, too. When he said he was a Christian, I was so ashamed that I felt I wasn't worth a cent. He would have helped me gladly even knowing the truth. I was wet with perspiration. Disgusted with myself, I kicked the wall of the terminal, and my foot ached for a long time afterwards.

There at the corner of the terminal I confessed my cowardice to God and prayed for forgiveness and asked for another chance. I promised God that when this chance came, I would not tell even one insignificant white lie. I was through with even well-intentioned lies.

Another chance did come. In the first part of June my family and I moved to San Francisco from the Topaz Relocation Center because I was appointed to reopen the San Francisco Japanese Methodist Church. I was to care for the Japanese returnees in the Bay Area until the time was ripe for the reopening of the church. Although war with Japan was still going on, Japanese were beginning to return quietly. Tension was still acute.

Fortunately, there were many Chinese in San Francisco. Caucasians (and sometimes Asians, for that matter) could not tell the difference between Chinese and Japanese. Very few Caucasians knew that Japanese were returning.

Alameda was also in my charge at that time. Alameda is a little town in the Bay Area, several miles away from San Francisco, and an important naval base. It was dangerous for me to go to Alameda even though it was no longer a restricted zone. Nevertheless I had to go there once in a while to see a few Japanese people living in the church building.

One day I was in Alameda, and about 9:00 P.M. I left the church. I chose this particular hour because I knew that not many people were going to San Francisco around that time. I had to walk several blocks to take the San Francisco bus. Naturally I chose a dark and quiet street. I was walking fast.

Suddenly I heard a shout, "Hey, you there! Stop!" I looked around and saw a navy man approaching. I thought he was one of the naval police.

"Where are you going?" he asked.

I thought it was the start of an investigation. "I am going to San Francisco, sir," I said.

"San Francisco, eh? I'll go with you." He had a rather commanding voice.

Naturally I believed that he would take me to the headquarters of the navy in San Francisco and would examine me thoroughly.

He paid my bus fare and sat beside me in the bus. I was extremely uncomfortable. There were only ten or eleven people in the bus when it started.

I could not imagine why he was taking me to the San Francisco headquarters. I had been walking on a dark street, but I had not been doing anything wrong.

"Sir, why are you taking me to San Francisco?" I asked.

He seemed rather surprised by my question. "I'm not taking you to San Francisco. You are taking me."

Now I was completely confused. "Why am I taking you to San Francisco?" I asked.

"I have never been there. I don't know the way; so I am following you."

"Is that all, sir?"

"Yes, that's all."

I began to feel better. Then I started to wonder about him as a person. He had a southern accent, which always interested me.

"I think you came here from somewhere down South," I said.

He did not answer.

"I'll bet you are from Texas," I said, speaking in the southern accent I learned when I was in school in Dallas.

He smiled at me. "Yes, I was born in Fort Worth, Texas," he said, "but this time I did not come from Texas. To tell the truth, our carrier was damaged by Jap planes in the South Pacific, so we returned to Alameda for repairs. The repairs will take forty-eight hours to be done. And I tell you, when our carrier is in good shape again, we will destroy every Jap plane and ship and kill every one of those damn Japs!"

I had been a big fool again asking such a question. I should have kept quiet. We rode in silence for a time.

The change was so extreme that he began to suspect me. "You are a Chinese, aren't you?" he asked.

I really wanted to say I was a Chinese. I knew I could avoid trouble that way because he was not an inquisitive man like that Chinese. However, I had promised God that I was through with lies. My answer to the navy man would be an answer to God as well.

"No, I am not a Chinese; I am a Japanese," I said.

He was greatly shocked when he realized that he had told a Japanese a secret of the navy. For a moment he seemed to have forgotten that he was in America, far from the battle front. I could see his rage mount as he raised both hands as if to choke me. It was as if a cat were about to catch a mouse. Yes, he was the cat, and I was the mouse.

I shouted, "*Mateh!*" meaning "wait a minute." The Japanese word came out automatically. Then I said in English, "Wait a minute. I am a minister of Jesus Christ, a servant of God." That was all I could say at that moment.

He heard me but was still in a rage. I closed my eyes and prayed to God to help me. When I opened my eyes, his hands were down.

"Are you really a minister of Christ?" he asked in a soft voice.

"Yes, I am."

He finally smiled at me again. "I am glad you are a Christian minister," he said. "I never thought that a Jap . . . Japanese, would be in Alameda. Reverend, I am not supposed to tell anyone about our carrier. Please don't let it be known that we are in Alameda for repair because this is supposed to be a secret."

"I promise you that I will keep it a secret until the war is over," I said.

"Thank you, Reverend," he said. "Reverend, I am a Christian myself."

I was so glad to hear that. "If you are a Christian," I said, "you know the Lord's Prayer, don't you?"

"Yes, I certainly do."

"Then let's pray the Lord's Prayer here in this running bus," I said. And we prayed together, "Our Father, who art in heaven . . . and forgive us our trespasses as we forgive those who trespass against us."

We both stopped there. We wiped our tears and then completed the last sentence. When we finished the Lord's Prayer, he and I were not enemies any longer; we were brothers before God.

"Are you married?" I asked.

"Yes, I am."

"Do you have children?"

"Yes, two children."

"Do you have their pictures with you?"

"Yes, I have a picture right here." He brought out a picture from his wallet and showed it to me.

"You have a beautiful wife and lovely children. I know you

would like to see them."

"Yes, very much. I miss them a lot. If the repairs had taken four days, I would have been able to see them, but I have only two days. I certainly miss them," he said.

I tried to cheer him. "I assure you that you will come back to your family soon. Have hope."

"Why are you so sure that I will come back alive?" he asked.

"For two reasons. One is that I will be praying for you every day until the war is over. The second reason is that the war is coming to an end now. I don't think there will be another severe sea battle in the South Pacific."

"Thank you, Reverend. You encourage me a great deal. Please remember me and my family in your prayers."

The bus reached San Francisco; it took only thirty-five minutes. When I said to him, "Goodbye and God bless you," he thanked me and, opening his wallet, handed me a five-dollar bill.

"I know this is not a big offering for your church," he said. "I want to do more, but I have the family to support. This is the very best I can do at this moment. Someday I hope to do better."

This was another inspiring experience in my life. When a little white lie grew into a chain of lies, I was very much ashamed of myself, but this time the truth brought me a great blessing.

21

The Mother Church Is Reopened

I have told that in the first part of June, 1945, before the end of the war, I returned to San Francisco with my family because I was appointed to reopen the Japanese Methodist Church, which is the mother church of all the Japanese Methodist churches in America, and to care for the Japanese returning from the centers. The two flats in the building in back of the church, one of which was the parsonage, were rented out to Caucasian families for unreasonably low rentals. Although the occupants in the parsonage had been asked to vacate the flat, they were still there when we arrived.

The sanctuary in the church building was rented out to the Fellowship Church of All Peoples. The fellowship hall and the rest of the building were filled with the furniture and other belongings that had been stored by the former church members before the evacuation. We found a small room in the corner of the fellowship hall that formerly had been used as a church office. That would be the temporary bedroom for the four of us—my wife, our nine-month-old daughter, my mother-in-law, and myself. We would use the church kitchen and bath on the top floor of the rear building. The arrangement did not seem much of a problem to us because any accommodation would be better than the horse stall we had been in at the Tanforan Assembly Center. However, we did not expect to live in this setup for as long as six months. The tenant would not vacate the parsonage, and we did not want to evict the family.

145

A few days after our return to San Francisco, two issei former church members, a man and a woman, returned to help us prepare the place for a small hostel, which the War Relocation Authority wanted us to open. The four or five rooms on the top floor of the rear building were cleaned, and the stored properties in the fellowship hall were moved to one side to make room for the army cots sent by the War Relocation Authority. Our hostel was mainly for women. Most of them stayed for a short time until they could find jobs.

We could not reopen the Japanese Methodist Church in San Francisco for seven months. One reason was that the Fellowship Church of All Peoples, who were renting our sanctuary, could not find a suitable building to move to. Another reason was that the well-meaning commission composed of the representatives of some of the Bay Area Protestant denominations tried to prevent the reopening of the Japanese churches. Their point was that the evacuation occurred because the Japanese were segregated; from now on our goal must be integration; there must be no Japanese churches. They were trying to do what they thought was best for the Japanese. Dr. Frank Herron Smith, Superintendent of the Japanese Provisional Conference of the Methodist Church at the time, was strongly opposed to this idea. He knew the Japanese churches and the Japanese people well. He insisted that it was not the time for integration—the Japanese churches needed to be reopened. The Protestant commission knew that I was determined to reopen the San Francisco church and would not give in to their pressure. It was no surprise, then, that I was criticized as a troublemaker.

When the Fellowship Church of All Peoples found a new place of worship and returned the sanctuary to us, I made preparations for the reopening of our church with the assistance of a few former church members. Our services in the hostel were almost coming to an end. Most of our former church members had relocated to the eastern part of the United States, and only a handful had returned to San Francisco at the time of our reopening. However, I decided to reopen the church as a nisei church, in other words, as an English-language church because I had heard that quite a number of nisei had returned or come into the city.

We asked the Japanese-American Citizens League, which had reopened its office in San Francisco to give assistance to the returnees, to provide us with the names and addresses of the nisei in San Francisco. To these we sent a formal printed announcement of the reopening of our church under the new name of Pine Methodist Church. I chose the name "pine," not only because the church was located on Pine Street, but also because the word "pine" is highly regarded by the Japanese for its meaning of long life and dignity. I also wrote letters to the Caucasian Methodist churches in the city asking them to give us moral support by sending two representatives from each church to worship with the nisei congregation on the day of our reopening. Among the former members who had returned there were not enough men to serve as ushers (in those days we did not think of having women serve as ushers); so my wife telephoned across the Bay to the Alameda church to ask several nisei men to come to help us.

On that first Sunday in January, 1946, when the doors of the old San Francisco church on Pine Street reopened for the 11 A.M. services, we had no idea what the response would be. We felt impatient anticipation, but we had faith. Then they started to arrive—nisei returnees in their neat Sunday attire, more women than men. It was thrilling to see them come to church: the small number of our former church members; the young women from our hostel. The nisei returnees from our Alameda church, six or seven, were there to help us; several Caucasian Methodists were there to encourage us; and many young nisei whom we did not know came, responding to our announcement and invitation. The congregation numbered more than 100. The Caucasians were surprised to see rows and rows of young adults, for most of the nisei at that time were in the young-adult age bracket.

Dr. Smith had told me, "Unless you get at least twenty-five families, you cannot keep this historic church open."

So we worked hard under the motto "The Church with a Growing Vision." In early April of that year services for the Japanese-language congregation started on Sunday afternoons. We started the choir, the young adult fellowship, the Sunday school, the midweek activities, the women's society.

We held fellowship luncheons and various special programs. The church was organized. The historic church could remain open and became financially independent.

When I left San Francisco in the summer of 1950 for my new appointment in Spokane, Washington, two ministers succeeded me: a promising, young nisei minister and a Japanese language minister. In 1965, under new ministerial leadership, the congregation built a beautiful church building in the Golden Gate Park area and moved there. They kept the name Pine Methodist Church.

This period in San Francisco was spiritually rewarding and enriching, not only in terms of ministry but to our family as well for it was in this period, on October 13, 1948, that our son, Justin Yoshito, was born. God blessed us with another precious gift.

22
The Letter to My Father

When World War II ended on August 15, 1945, my first concern was for the welfare of my father. I did not even know whether he was still alive.

American newspapers had reported that practically all of the large cities in Japan had been bombed and destroyed by the B-29s. I knew that Kyoto, the ancient cultural center of Japan, had not been bombed because of General MacArthur's decision to preserve this beautiful and historic city. Kanazawa, where my father lived, was called a little Kyoto, but I had no way of knowing whether or not it too had been spared. There were no means of communication immediately after the war.

Soon after General MacArthur entered Tokyo, one of my Alameda church members, Roy Teshima, was sent to Japan as an interpreter. Through him I was able to discover that my father was still living. Roy wrote me that my father had been told I was killed by an American soldier soon after the outbreak of the war. He could scarcely believe Roy's news that I was well and living in San Francisco.

As I knew my father was undernourished, I wanted more than anything to send him a package of food. This I was able to do through Roy. When my father received the eleven-pound package of rice and sugar, he wept over it. He had not seen white rice or sugar for years.

Soon after that we were allowed to send eleven-pound packages directly to people in Japan; later the amount was increased to twenty-one pounds. I sent my father package after

149

package, about eighty pounds a month, which he was able to share with his neighbors. Later, when postal money orders were permitted, I sent him thirty dollars a month.

During this period after the war I was personally wrestling with a serious moral and ethical problem. It caused me days of worry and sleepless nights, and for many years I was not sure that I finally reached the right decision.

My problem was whether to return to Japan or to stay in America. Where did my highest duty lie?

When I first came to America, I didn't have the slightest idea of remaining permanently. I had intended to go back as soon as my studies were finished. Before the war, while I was serving as a student pastor in Alameda, Dr. Smith, the superintendent, had advised me to change my student's status to that of a minister and remain in America for good. But soon the war broke out.

One day while in San Francisco, I received a letter from the Reverend Hoitsu Kimura, formerly one of the most important Methodist ministers in Japan. (All denominations were united and organized into the Nippon United Church shortly before the outbreak of the war. There is no Methodist Church, as such, in Japan today.)

The Reverend Mr. Kimura's letter said in part, "Japan needs you. I believe you can do better service to God and the people here in Japan than in America. Unfortunately, many capable ministers in Japan had to make some compromise with the militarists during the war days. But you have no dark spot. You can go to General MacArthur's headquarters without fear. We need you. Come back to Japan and help those Japanese who are in deep despair."

When I read his letter, my heart was deeply moved. I felt that I must go back to Japan. Japan was my country. (I was not naturalized then; America did not even have the present naturalization law for Japanese.) Her people were my people. It was my duty and privilege to suffer with them. If I did not return, I would be a traitor to Japan. Yes, I would go back to my nation and my people as soon as possible.

I went to our new superintendent, Dr. Richardson, explained my situation, and asked his opinion. He said that he needed me here in America because the Japanese people on the West Coast were also in deep despair. Most of them had lost everything during the war and had to start all over again. If I left them now, they would think that I left the wandering sheep in the wilderness. He emphatically said that he would not permit me to go back to Japan. My heart became heavier and heavier.

I asked my wife's advice. "If it's for the kingdom of God, I'll go with you wherever you go," she said.

I had expected this sort of answer. She knew that life in Japan would not be easy or pleasant for her. Her words, even though expected, moved me deeply.

"But how about our two-year-old daughter? Do you think she would be happy in Japan?" I asked my wife.

"Gloria is a small child," she said. "I'm sure she will be able to adjust to any circumstance; so don't worry about me and our daughter. Decide whatever you think best in the sight of God."

After this encouragement from my wife, I almost decided to go back to Japan. Still I hesitated. I reconsidered the matter more carefully and analyzed the situation more thoughtfully.

The focus came to my daughter again. I thought to myself, *She is our only daughter. We waited six years for her coming. For her, America is much, much better than Japan in every way. And she is an American citizen. If I took her to Japan, and if she were not happy there, I could not stand it. I know there are many great ministers who do not pay much attention to their children and spend all their time and energy on evangelistic work. They have become great ministers, but I cannot be that way. To take part in forming the horizon of the new Japan is an attractive picture, but to me my family must come first. If I cannot be a good father to my daughter and a good husband to my wife, then I cannot be a good minister either. I will stay in America and work in America, taking good care of my daughter and my wife and my people here who are starting their new life from the bottom.*

When I told my wife about my final decision, she was rather happy about it and promised her full support of my work in America. And yet I myself was not wholly sure I had done the right thing.

I wrote to the Reverend Mr. Kimura and begged him to understand my decision. He replied immediately, saying, "I understand your situation. I will not ask you anymore about coming back. Do your best to serve the people in America. However, one thing I will ask you. Please remember the churches and ministers in Japan in your prayers and help them by sending food, clothes, medicine, and other daily necessities."

I felt that I was released from a heavy burden. Responding to his appeal, I sent more packages. Everything I sent was needed and appreciated by the people there. My financial ability was limited; so I asked many churches and organizations, both Caucasian and Japanese, to send packages to churches and ministers in Japan. A great number of churches in America sent many good things, new and used, to me in San Francisco and asked me to forward them to Japan. Our Pacific Japanese Provisional Conference paid about $1,000 for postage and other expenses.

The things sent to me included suits, dresses, sweaters, shoes, top coats, trousers, blankets, sheets, towels, soap, toothpaste, medicine, canned foods, raisins, sugar, salt, rice, flour, stockings, gloves, handkerchiefs, safety pins, needles, thread, yarn, notebooks, crayons, coloring books for children, and much more. I also bought about 100 used suits at the Goodwill Industry in San Francisco with money received from the Japanese Provisional Conference.

I could not handle all these things alone; so I called on the church members. They helped by wrapping and addressing packages and taking them to the post offices.

I sent two-thirds of these supplies to the Reverend Mr. Manabe, a leader of the Japan United Church in Tokyo, asking him to distribute them among the ministers and churches in eastern Japan, and the other one-third to the Reverend Mr. Kimura for western Japan. I sent quite a few packages to the Hiroshima Girls' Institute because some churches requested that their gifts go there.

The Reverend Mr. Kimura wrote to me, saying, "Many ministers were strengthened and blessed by your services."

Bishop Abe, the former Methodist bishop, was one of the

earliest visitors to America after the war. When he came to my church in San Francisco, he showed me his suit and said, "You know, this is one of the suits you sent to Mr. Manabe in Tokyo. He gave it to me when he heard I was going to America. Thank you, Mr. Shimada."

In 1949 I had a chance to visit Japan. One of my church members operated a traveling bureau. He was organizing a tour of Japan, for which he needed a leader. He offered me the job. All my expenses would be paid.

It was a wonderful chance for me. I had been hoping for just such an opportunity; when it came, I found that I lacked the courage to go. My thoughts ran this way: *Are you able to meet all your minister friends who have gone through all kinds of suffering and pain and trouble for the reestablishment of their churches in Japan in the midst of a shortage of everything? You were supposed to return and share their suffering, but you stayed in America where you have everything. Yes, you had your good reasons for staying, and you excuse yourself for those personal reasons, but your friends in Japan may not think they were so valid. They may think you are a coward. You have no face to meet them. You had better give up this chance and hide yourself behind the Pacific Ocean.*

And so I did not go.

Through all of this period my thoughts were also with my father. One day in the spring of 1951 in Spokane, where we had moved the previous year, I had an idea that I discussed with my wife.

"When I was young," I said, "I made a promise to God. I promised him that if he would keep my father in his hand while I could not take care of him, I would convert him to Christianity. God has certainly done his part. He has kept my father in his hand not only while I was studying in Japan and in America but also during and after the war. Now the time has come for me to keep my promise. If I cannot convert my father to Christianity, I am a false prophet. This is a challenge I must accept."

We decided to invite my father to America. At that time we had only forty dollars in the bank. We had faith, however, that God would provide the way if the coming of my father was God's will.

Within two years we were able to save $350, which was enough for a one-way sea fare. I wrote a letter to my father.

My dear Father:
My wife and I have decided to invite you to America for the following reasons:

1. Ever since I became a parent myself, I have realized what a wonderful father you have been and what an unworthy son I have been to you. I want to see your face so I can tell you this personally.

2. I want you to see America, the Christian nation, with your own eyes. You were an educator, and thus you have the eyes to see why America is such a wonderful nation. And I want you also to see my Christian home and my life as a minister. I am trying to do my best as a minister, just as you did your best as a teacher.

3. Please give me a chance to explain Christianity to you. If you come to the conclusion that Christianity is the best religion, please let me baptize you. However, if you still believe that Buddhism is the best religion, it will be all right with me. I know that faith should not be forced.

4. I have two children, a daughter and a son. They want very much to see their grandfather; so please come to America to meet your grandchildren.

I knew my father well. I realized that he would not pay much attention to the first three points, but I thought that he could not ignore the last. I hoped he would come to America to see his grandchildren.

I was right. He did not care about religion, but he was deeply interested in seeing his grandchildren. However, one of my brothers tried to discourage him by telling him, "No, Father, you should not go to America because it is too far away. You are not strong enough and are still undernourished. I am afraid that you may die on the way. Do you know what will happen when you die on the ship? Your body will be wrapped with white cloth and thrown into the ocean, and some big fish will eat you up. I will not let you go to that far country. Please stay here in Japan."

My father, realizing that he was not strong, could not decide. In America, we did not know that such an argument was going on in Japan. We waited for his reply, but for five weeks we had no answer. After much contemplation, however, he decided to come.

"I don't care whether a big fish eats me or not," he said. "I want to see my grandchildren."

His letter finally reached us. My wife opened it and read: "Thank you for your invitation. I have made up my mind to come to America. See you all there."

"Goodness," my wife said, "his letter sounds like a telegram, doesn't it?"

It was at any rate a joyous and hopeful telegram for me.

23

The Promise to God Is Fulfilled

My father had taken so long in making up his mind about coming that he missed the ship; it was necessary for him to come on a plane. He arrived at the Seattle-Tacoma Airport on June 11, 1953. I stood on the balcony watching the landing. As the door of the plane opened, I was straining my eyes for a sight of him.

The moment a slight, aged figure came through the door, I knew it was the father I had not seen for twenty-five years. The moment I had longed for was almost at hand.

He was changed, of course. Although I could not see his face at that distance, he looked small and frail. I was not surprised. A week before, I had received a letter from my sister-in-law warning me not to be shocked by his appearance, as he had withered from undernourishment during the war years.

As he walked toward the immigration office I shouted in Japanese, "Father, Shigeo is here to meet you," and I waved at him.

He looked up and smiled as he entered the immigration office. Both of his hands were full; so he could not wave back. I wanted to see him immediately, without waiting for the custom inspection; so I went right down to the immigration office. The door was open; I went right in.

"Hey, where are you going?" An inspector blocked my path.

"I want to see my father," I said.

"No. Nobody comes in until the examinations are over."

"I'm not going to do anything wrong; I just want to see my father. I am a minister."

"Even if you were God," the inspector said, "I will not permit you to come into this room until the examinations are finished. Go and wait outside."

I made one last attempt. "My father's formal Japanese is difficult to understand," I said. "You will need me as an interpreter."

"There is nothing the matter with our interpreter. Don't worry so much. Just go back outside and wait for about an hour."

There was no moving the man. I returned to the waiting room and tried to be patient. In about ten minutes the loudspeaker announced: "Will the Reverend Mr. Shimada please come to the immigration office." I went back to the office and was met by the same officer who would not have admitted God.

"Our interpreter is having a little trouble with your father's Japanese," he said. "Would you please help us?"

Apparently he had really meant that God would not be admitted unless God spoke formal Japanese. I smiled and said, "I told you it would be difficult." He smiled back and took me to the next room where my father was standing.

I wanted to embrace him, but I knew that would not be the Japanese way. I patted his shoulder softly. "Father," I said, "I will greet you later. I have a job here first." I thought that he understood me.

The immigration officer asked me questions about my father and myself. He didn't use me as an interpreter at all; he just asked me the questions. In a short time we were finished there, and my father had to go to the next room for another inspection. As there was a line and he looked so tired I took him to a chair at the side of the room and sat down with him.

This was the time for the warm greeting that I had so carefully prepared and memorized. I had even practiced it two or three times. Now I couldn't remember a word of it. In the emotion of the moment, my mind was a blank.

"Father, how was the airplane trip?" I had not intended my first words to be so meaningless.

My father surprised me by standing up, saluting me with a deep bow, and answering in formal Japanese: "I profoundly appreciate your kind question. Indeed I have enjoyed my airplane trip very much, sir."

I was shocked at the formal attitude and at the elaborate language that I would not have expected to hear from a close relative. I knew that Japan had changed after World War II, but I had never expected this much of a change. He was speaking to me as though I were his lord or master. I felt that I should speak to him in return as though he were an aristocrat. I stood up and bowed low before him.

"My sir, I am very happy to know that you have enjoyed your trip, sir," I said, also in formal Japanese.

We continued talking for a time, using the old classic Japanese language. My father was a schoolteacher and knew all the classic words; he certainly used a lot of them in that conversation. I was not comfortable at all. This was not the meeting I had been dreaming of. Then my father pointed upstairs.

"Sir," he said, "my son is waiting for me up there. Would you please find him for me?"

My father had not recognized me! I had called him "Father" several times, but his age had made him hard of hearing. He thought he was talking to a kind stranger.

After the first moment of shock I began to laugh. I realized that since coming to America I had put on weight—I had been very thin in Japan—and that my appearance was greatly changed. I had hoped to grow in height, but always I grew in the other direction. Sideways.

"Father," I said, "what's the big idea? I am your son, Shigeo."

He in turn was shocked and speechless for a moment. Then he too began to laugh.

"My goodness," he said, "you are so fat."

He now spoke in the most informal and intimate way, and everything was all right again.

Within thirty minutes all formalities were finished. I took my father to Seattle and put him in a comfortable bed in a good hotel. He was so tired that he fell immediately into a deep sleep. He started to snore, but it did not bother me at all. In fact, it was music to me. I thanked God from the bottom of my heart for his merciful hand upon my father, and I prayed to him to help me lead my father to Christianity.

The next day, right after breakfast, we left Seattle and started toward Spokane. My father admired my driving. He enjoyed the scenery; everything was interesting and new to him. He was amazed by the beautiful highways through the mountains and the valleys. In the car he sat on the seat with his legs folded in the Japanese way. He said that he was more comfortable like that.

As he was in such a happy mood, I thought it was a good opportunity for me to apologize for the wrong I had done him when I was young in Japan.

"My son," he said in a gentle voice, "everything has turned out to be fine now; so let us not go back to our old wounds. You are my pride. Not only my neighbors but many other people in Kanazawa respect you. They know your name even though they have never met you. My visiting America is big news in Kanazawa. You are not only my pride, but all Kanazawa city is proud of you today."

And so all old wounds were healed.

We arrived at the parsonage in Spokane an hour earlier than scheduled. My two excited children ran from the house shouting "Grandpa!" They spoke rather good Japanese at that time, with some American accent. My father was very pleased by their warm welcome. My mother-in-law greeted him in the old Japanese way, bowing several times. My father must have bowed more than ten times.

As we entered the house, my wife came down the stairs, smiling. She greeted him as if he were her own father. He brought some gifts to the children, Japanese books and toys. They were thrilled.

Our dinner time that evening was a happy occasion. My father enjoyed the ham. "I have never tasted such delicious pig meat in my life," he said.

After dinner I asked him to go to the prayer meeting of the Japanese-speaking congregation with me because the church members were expecting to see him there. He was willing to meet them. There were about fifty of the older generation present. At the beginning of the meeting I introduced him to them.

"This is my father. There are about three billion people on

the earth, but he is the only person in the world whom I can call my father. To me he is the most precious person in the whole world."

When I said this much, my father started weeping for joy, and some of the members shared his tears. I had not intended to make this meeting so sentimental; I wanted it to be bright and happy. I told them about my father mistaking me for an interpreter. They all laughed, and it turned out to be a cheerful gathering. Several members offered a prayer of thanksgiving for my father's safe arrival.

A few days later the church people held a welcome party for my father. It was a big occasion, and he said that he had never had such a warm reception in his life.

I had given a great deal of thought to the best method for leading my father to Christianity. I had seen the movie "Iwo Jima," and it gave me an idea.

Iwo Jima is a tiny island in the Pacific. It has no economic value, being useless for farming, fishing, industry, or mining. Yet it was vital to American strategy in the Pacific war. America used every possible resource against this tiny island, risking the heaviest casualties, because it was so important to them. In the movie I saw masses of ships, planes, and artillery in action, and finally thousands of marines dashing over the island like tidal waves, one wave after the other. In the end five heroic marines placed the American flag on Suribachi Hill.

My father was my Iwo Jima. He was small in stature and did not hold any important position in the world. He was not wealthy. Nevertheless, to my ministerial work he was Iwo Jima. If I could lead him to Christianity, my life as a minister would have meaning and success.

After seeing the movie I decided that was the answer. I would bring every resource to bear. I would overwhelm him by mobilizing all the manpower I had.

All the members of my family, and my church members as well, did their part. My children showed him pictures and books about Jesus, explaining the text in their American-Japanese which he, a typical grandfather, thought was cute. He enjoyed doing anything with the children. My mother-in-law told him how she accepted Christianity and how she was baptized by Dr. Toyohiko Kagawa when he came to Santa Barbara. My wife showered him with Christian love and kindness, which he appreciated deeply.

My church members remembered my father in their daily prayers and showed kindness in countless ways. My father began to feel the warmth of Christian love. He started to join the Sunday worship services. He did this of his own accord. My Sunday sermons were aimed at my father, and the church members knew this and approved it.

My church gave me a month vacation and advised me to take my father to visit places of interest on the West Coast. He enjoyed everything; his enthusiasm made me feel that I was seeing the country with new eyes.

He looked at Grand Coulee Dam with amazement and was even more impressed when I explained how the dam held a vast volume of water, stretching a hundred miles to the north.

"Ah," he said, "What a richly blessed nation America is, and what a poor country Japan is in material things."

At Mount Rainier, where we drove up almost 7,000 feet in the car, he said: "My goodness! It is unbelievable that I climbed a high mountain while sitting down."

This led us to a recollection of the time when I was a high school student and my father and I climbed a 3,000-foot mountain. It almost took fifteen hours. The mountain was ten miles from our home, and we had to walk both ways because there was no convenient bus or train. To my father climbing mountains meant walking; so he was astonished to climb 7,000 feet in a car.

Driving along the Columbia River he looked at the towering cliffs and deep ravines and shook his head. "I feel as though I am traveling in dreamland. It is absolutely impossible to see such unique scenes in Japan."

At Yosemite National Park he was bewildered by the huge rocks and giant trees. "I feel like a dwarf. Everything here is so big!"

In Santa Barbara he was interested in the Spanish atmosphere. At the court house, built in Spanish style, he said, "Is this still America?"

At Forest Lawn Cemetery in Los Angeles his first reaction

was: "Is this really a cemetery? I thought it was a public park."

I took him through the cemetery; he was deeply impressed by the great picture of Christ just before the crucifixion. I explained to him that Jesus Christ, the Son of God, had to be crucified on the cross because of our sins, and because of this sacrificial death on the cross the way of salvation was opened to all the people in the world.

While he listened to me, he looked closely at the picture. I knew he was impressed. Forest Lawn was the last stop of our sightseeing.

We started to return to San Francisco where my family was waiting to join us again. My father was very quiet in the car.

"Is something wrong?" I asked.

"Oh, no. Nothing is wrong; everything is more than fine."

About halfway to San Francisco my father said to me, "My son, I have been thinking since I first came to America. Is it too late for me to become a Christian?"

"No, Father, it is never too late to become a child of God."

At last my prayer of twenty-five years was answered. My heart was so filled with thanksgiving that I had no words to utter. We rode the rest of the way in silence and in deep thought.

On August 30, Father was asked to broadcast his impression of America over one of the Spokane radio stations. He spoke in Japanese, and I interpreted.

In his broadcast my father said, "America is a wonderful nation. Highways are like a web. Every city has an airport. The educational system is almost perfect. Social security and welfare services are wonderful. People have plenty of food. In Japan, just to live is a difficult task, but here in America people enjoy life.

"I find that Christianity has a great influence in every field in America—in education, social affairs, business, and even politics. Here in America the people I have encountered in the post offices, banks, and department stores are kind and polite. I have been especially impressed by the humble attitude of government officials and people with high positions. I certainly believe that they are influenced by the teachings of Christ.

"I was a grade school teacher, and I taught my pupils that

Christianity was a wicked religion. I once believed that myself. Now I realize that I was wrong. I have discovered that Christianity is a wonderful religion on which this great nation has been founded.

"I have made a decision to become a Christian. Next Sunday I will be baptized by my son in his church, and when I return to Japan, I will do my small share in establishing God's kingdom in my country."

September 6, 1953, was the day of my father's baptism. It was an ordinary Sunday; everything was as usual. Yet, it was the most significant day in my life. That day I fulfilled my promise to God.

The baptism took place during the afternoon service of the Japanese language congregation. About seventy-five people were present. Seven or eight Caucasians also attended even though they could not understand Japanese. They asked me to allow them to join the service. They said they had heard my father's radio talk and wanted to be present. They were, of course, very welcome.

When the time came for the baptism, my father came forward and knelt down before me. I took the ritual book and started to read calmly. I was neither excited nor nervous at the beginning. Everything went smoothly. But when I put my hand upon his head and called his name, "Tatsutaro Shimada," not as his son but as his minister, I suddenly felt a lump in my throat; I lost my voice. I struggled to read from the ritual book, but I could not. Tears began to roll down my cheeks. Overcome by emotion, I stood there helpless.

I prayed silently, "Help me, God. I must be calm. This is the most important day of my life. Please help me, O God."

After my prayer I regained control of myself. My voice filled the silent sanctuary: "I baptize thee in the name of the Father, and of the Son, and of the Holy Spirit."

I was not satisfied with the way I conducted the baptismal service. I felt that I had done a poor job, and I was sorry for my father, who deserved better. As I stood at the door after the service to greet the congregation, my heart was heavy.

One of the Caucasian women who attended the service said to me, "I have seen many baptismal services in my life, but today I saw the most sincere and beautiful of them all. I shall never forget this meaningful baptism as long as I live."

My church members also told me that they were impressed by my father's baptism; they said it was the most inspiring service ever held in that church.

In spite of all their kind words, I still doubted that I had been worthy of this wonderful ceremony. After all the members were gone, I asked my wife to tell me frankly what she thought of the service.

She smiled at me. "It was a beautiful service. Once you and your father were a million miles apart, but the moment you baptized him you became one in heart and in faith. That was the moment you fulfilled the promise to God you made twenty-five years ago."

And then my heart was light and cheerful. When my wife told me it was a good service after all, I believed her.

That evening we had a happy dinner table. To me my father looked like a new person. My gratitude for this wonderful blessing bestowed upon my life was beyond words.

When the picture of my father's baptism appeared in the local newspapers, I received many telephone calls and letters from unknown Christian friends. Practically all of them mentioned the same point. "We believe now that Jesus Christ is really living today and continues to work through us." Their calls and letters warmed my heart.

The time came for my father to return to Japan. This time he wanted to take a ship rather than a plane. During his four-month visit in America, he had gained seven pounds and looked healthier and years younger. Thus there was no more worry about being eaten by fish in the middle of the Pacific Ocean.

The day he left for Spokane, he expressed his deepest appreciation to my wife and to my children. He said to my wife, "Even my own daughter would not be able to take care of me as you have done. Thank you very much indeed."

He wept when she hugged him as though he were her own father.

We had to go to San Francisco to get on the ship. My father wanted to see other famous and historic places on the way. I took him to Salt Lake, Brice Canyon, Zion National Park, and the Grand Canyon.

On the rim of the Grand Canyon he said, "What an unusual scene. It's like looking down into a grand hell."

On the way to California from the Grand Canyon he was amazed at the giant cactus of the Arizona desert. He was fond of cactus plants and kept several of them in pots at home; he thought all cactus were small. He suddenly shouted, "Wow!" (An expression he picked up from my children.) "Cactus, cactus!" He had thought at first that they were electric or telephone poles. He asked me to stop the car so he could take pictures.

San Francisco ended our trip. Before he embarked I took him to the Golden Gate Park and showed him the Japanese garden there. "This garden makes me homesick," he said.

"I'm glad you didn't get homesick until the end of your trip."

He smiled. "People in Spokane were so kind that I had no chance to become homesick there."

This comment made me happy. Everything about my father's visit made me happy. Four months before he had been an old, shrunken man, wearing a shabby suit, but now he looked young and handsome. Most important of all, he was returning to Japan as a baptized Christian.

On the ship I said to him, "Father, as you know, I came to America as a student, not as a minister. I meant to go back to Japan, but I have stayed in America. Now I want you to take my place in Japan and do your best for Christ and his kingdom. I know you cannot become a minister, but as far as spirit is concerned, I want you to take my place in Japan."

He agreed. My next statement was impulsive.

"One more thing, Father. In 1959, Japanese Protestants will celebrate their 100th anniversary. I will visit Japan then and hold an evangelistic meeting in Kanazawa. I want you to preside at my meeting there."

"I will do it."

It was time for me to leave the ship. As I held my father's hand, we could not say a word; our hearts were filled with emotion. I stood at the dock until the ship disappeared from sight.

And I wondered if I would find the courage to return to Japan in 1959.

24

My Brother Finds New Life at Forty

In 1954, I had a second chance to visit Japan. My church members gave me a three-month leave of absence and $500 to use as I saw fit. This was not enough for the trip, but it was enough for a start. I knew that if I mentioned a desire to go to Japan, my church members would encourage me to do so. I was tempted.

In the end and for the same reasons as before—reluctance to face my brother ministers in Japan after what I thought they might consider my desertion in their time of need—I did not go. I went to the Perkins School of Theology of Southern Methodist University and studied for three months, taking refresher courses in theology and the New Testament. It was a valuable experience, but it was not meeting the challenge. I still did not know what I would do at the time of the 100th anniversary in 1959.

Aside from my father, other problems of my family in Japan had been of concern to me since just after the war. My brother Takeo had only one child, a daughter. At about the age of six she became seriously ill.

Takeo asked me to send medicines that were not available in Japan at that time, and I did so, but nothing did any good. The child died in 1947. To my brother it was the end of everything. His daughter had been a lovely girl—brilliant and talented—and he could not forget her. His wife managed to face the situation with more courage.

I wrote one letter of encouragement after another, but my

letters did not help him. He became more and more despondent.

In 1953, after my father returned from America, he visited Takeo. He wrote to me immediately, telling me how concerned he was over Takeo's despondency. My father urged me to do something about my brother; if I could not, he was not hopeful for the future.

I talked this over with my wife, as I do all my problems. We decided to invite Takeo to America for a year of study. We hoped the change would benefit him. We knew that it would be a great financial burden, but we profoundly believed that reviving one soul would be more important than any material treasure.

I wrote to Takeo, who was interested in the idea. He started to brush up on the little English he had learned in school. He began to have hope. He spent a year and a half preparing for the trip. The Educational Department of Osaka granted him a year's leave of absence.

When he went to the American consulate in Kobe to get a visa for his passport, the American consul would not give it to him. The consul said that forty years of age was too old to go to America for study. Takeo was extremely disappointed and wrote to me for guidance.

I wrote to him that while it was true he was older than the usual student, he must accept that fact and overcome it. I then wrote a speech for him, in English, and told him to go again to the American consulate and make the speech to the consul.

As much as I can remember of what I wrote ran like this: "Moses in the Old Testament started his new life at the age of forty. If he could do that why can't I? Moses and I believe in the same God, the Creator. If there is a definite rule that a person over forty cannot study in America, then I must give up hope. If there is no such rule, please open the door for me to start a new life."

My brother memorized every word of that statement and went to the American consulate again. His wife, who was also a school teacher (and better in English than Takeo) memorized it, too, and went to the consulate with him. As Takeo stood before the consul and repeated the words, Keiko stood beside him and helped him whenever he got stuck. Takeo wrote to me that this time the consul seemed impressed by his appeal and granted the visa willingly.

I was amused by the story; I had not expected them to follow my advice so literally.

Thus Takeo came to America in the summer of 1955. I met him at the Seattle-Tacoma Airport as I had met my father, and I was curious to see whether he would recognize me. The moment he saw me he waved at me; so we had no problem that way.

Takeo studied at Whitworth College in Spokane for a year. The language handicap made things difficult for him, but he worked hard. As a teacher, he enjoyed the education courses the most. He lived with us and helped the church choir in our Japanese language division. His relationship with the church members was warm and satisfying to him.

After a year of study in this Christian college, Takeo returned to Japan. He was a completely changed man, a new man, full of hope and enthusiasm for life.

He was the only teacher in the junior high schools of Osaka who had studied in America. Soon after his return home he was made dean of students in his school and later vice-principal. He was appointed to the committee working with juvenile delinquents and became one of the authorities on the problem of delinquency in Osaka.

My wife and I were happy that we had been able to contribute something toward his renewed interest in life.

25

A Church Rises on the Rock

An experience that has meant much to me has been the growth and development of our church in Spokane, where I had been pastor since 1950. An important part of this growth had been our new building, which is our pride.

The church had bought the old church building in Spokane from the Swedish Methodist congregation about thirty years before. It was adequate when I first arrived, but five years later we needed to expand. We decided to build a new church.

We realized that about $75,000 would be the maximum we could raise. We planned to get two-thirds of this from the members and friends of the church; one-third was promised as a donation from the Division of National Missions of the Board of Missions of the Methodist Church, whose headquarters was in Philadelphia.

The building committee located a piece of rocky land about five blocks east of our old church. This land was owned by the City of Spokane. The board asked me to negotiate with the city for its purchase.

The man I dealt with was Mr. Emmett Lancaster, the city treasurer. He was a very friendly gentleman with a pleasant smile. In our conversation I was surprised to hear him use several Japanese words.

"Have you ever been in Japan?" I asked.

"No, although I would like to visit there someday."

"How did you learn to speak Japanese?"

"Well, when I was young, I had a very good Japanese friend.

He was the minister of your church then. I taught him English, and he taught me Japanese. I still remember some easy Japanese words. I like to have Japanese people in Spokane. They are honest, sincere, and hardworking people. I have much respect for them and have been hoping to do something for them, but I haven't had the chance."

I then explained my congregation's wish to buy that piece of land. I told him we could not afford to pay a high price.

"If you people want to build a house of God on those vacant lots," Mr. Lancaster said, "I will make it very reasonable for you. There are nineteen lots altogether. The city has kept that land for fifty-two years, but so far no one has tried to buy it because it is so rough and rocky. You are our first customer. I will offer you the lowest price, $2,865 for nineteen lots. How about it?"

I thought it was very reasonable even for land of that sort. I expressed my deep appreciation for his kindness.

"Won't you get into trouble for selling the land at such a low price?" I asked.

He smiled. "Don't you worry. I haven't done anything wrong before God or man. As you are building a house of God, I personally would like to give it to you free, but in my position I cannot do that."

I thanked God for the friendship between Mr. Lancaster and our former pastor, which brought us this blessing thirty years later. Thus we purchased the land.

On Easter afternoon, 1957, my congregation of children, youths, and adults gathered on the ugly, rocky land for the groundbreaking ceremony. It was a windy but sunny day.

During the ceremony the participants had a hard time breaking the ground because of the rocks. An old woman actually wept that we could only afford to buy this poor, miserable piece of land.

I realized that this building project was no easy task for my small congregation, most of whom had only modest incomes. This church could be built only by their love, faith, sacrifice, and effort. Erecting this house of God was a great challenge to me and to my congregation; it was the test of our Christian faith.

In the ruined city of Hiroshima the Christians of Nagare-gawa Church built a church before they built their own houses. Hiroshima Christians were all victims of the atomic bomb; they had lost everything. Some of them lost husbands, wives, parents, and children. They did not know where to find their next meal.

All the surviving members gathered in the ruined church with their pastor, the Reverend Mr. Kiyoshi Tanimoto, and prayed together and pledged to build a house of God in the midst of their poverty, sorrow, and suffering. They actually built their church in that devastated city before they built their own houses.

I told my church people, "We are not the victims of an atomic bomb. If we should fail in this project, our Christian faith is much weaker than the faith of the Hiroshima Christians. This is a challenge to us; this is the test of our Christian faith. Let us do our very best in erecting the house of God on the rock."

The money-raising campaign was the most difficult part of our building project. This important task was spearheaded by Mr. Masuo Akiyama for the English-speaking division and Mr. Umenosuke Kasai for the Japanese-speaking division. Both were dedicated and enthusiastic chairmen, and the work progressed well.

Then a crisis arose in the midst of the campaign. While I was away I received the shocking news that Mr. Kasai had died suddenly of a heart attack. His death was a great loss not only to our church but to the Japanese community in Spokane. He was an influential man, often referred to as the "mayor of the Japanese community." I knew that his death would be a blow to our building project.

From the beginning I had depended on him a great deal. He carried many of the heavy responsibilities and burdens of our project. He continually encouraged the Japanese-speaking issei, saying, "We are getting old. Soon we will go back to heaven. The building of our church may be our last service on the earth; let us do our utmost."

The Japanese community turned out for his funeral service to pay him their last tribute. After the service was over and the people were gone, his family and I gathered around the casket to bid him farewell.

While I was looking at his serene and peaceful face with my misty eyes, I felt as if he were speaking to me, "I am dead now; therefore you must stand on your own feet and take this responsibility and finish it. I will be watching you from heaven."

"Yes, Mr. Kasai," I said from my heart. "I will finish it. Watch me from heaven."

I rose with renewed courage and strength.

Our pledges reached the goal, and we received the generous donation of $25,000 from the headquarters, but the trouble was that while we were building, the prices of all materials and laborers' wages went up. Then of course improvements and changes occurred to us, all of which sent the cost higher.

We ran short of funds, and we had to start another fund-raising campaign. We called it the "Second-Mile Donation." However, our "second mile" did not work well for a while, and I was afraid we had come to the bottom of the barrel. Then a miracle happened.

One day I went to Hood River, Oregon, hoping to raise some money among a few Japanese friends there. I stayed two days in the home of Mr. and Mrs. Iwatsuki. Mrs. Iwatsuki took me to visit three Japanese families in Hood River, from whom I received $300. It was much better than I had expected.

Then Mr. and Mrs. Iwatsuki donated $300. It was more than wonderful. The next day I came back to Spokane with a happy feeling because after all I had raised $600 in Hood River in two days.

Mr. Iwatsuki was one of the most inspiring Christian personalities I had ever met. Several years before my visit he fell from a cherry tree on his ranch, and since then he had spent his days in a wheelchair. He was partially paralyzed, yet he never complained about his accident. He took it as a trial from God and patiently waited for the day when he would be strengthened. He had a strong faith that someday, with the help of the living Christ, he would be able to walk again.

A few days after I returned home a letter from Mr. Iwatsuki reached me. When I opened it, a check fell out. I picked it up and at first glance thought the amount was $200. I thought for an instant that someone in Hood River wanted to make an anonymous donation and had asked Mr. Iwatsuki to send it to me.

I put my glasses on and started to read the letter. It was written by Mr. Iwatsuki himself; he must have spent more than two hours writing that one page with his partially paralyzed hand. He said in his letter:

Dear Rev. Shimada:

Your visit brought to us such a joy and blessing that we cannot forget it for a long time. When you were about to leave us yesterday morning, my wife and I felt something warm in our hearts. After you left, we both believed that you had come as the representative of Christ. We have some money that we saved for our new church building in Hood River. But the official board finally decided that we would not build because of the small Japanese population in this area.

My wife and I feel that the money we saved is no longer ours but belongs to God. We came to the conclusion that the best thing to do is to donate it to the new house of God that you are building in Spokane.

So herewith we enclose a check for $2,000 with faith, hope, and love. Would you please accept it and use it wherever you need it in your project?

Sincerely yours,
Kamegoro Iwatsuki

As I read his letter, my body started to tremble and my heart beat fast, not because the amount was $2,000 but because I really believed that the living Christ was with me and was working for us. I was profoundly inspired by the letter, which made me even more earnest about this project.

This miracle encouraged our church members, and many offered their Second-Mile donations. The campaign was successful.

The new Highland Park Methodist Church was enhanced by its Japanese rock garden. It had been my dream since I came to America to build a unique church with a beautiful Japanese garden. When I was a little boy, I went to see the garden in Kenroku Park in my native town of Kanazawa. Kenroku Park used to be the garden of Lord Maeda, one of the richest lords in the feudalistic age. When the feudal system came to an end about 100 years ago, the Maeda family donated their garden to Kanazawa. Whenever I visited this garden during my boyhood days, I was inspired by the beauty of it and felt peace in my heart.

When I came to America in 1935, I noticed that American gardens are flower gardens whereas Japanese gardens are rock gardens; that American gardens are colorful but Japanese gardens are evergreen. I had always been convinced that any American who loves the American flower garden would also love a Japanese rock garden. From that time I felt that a church in America with a Japanese landscape might be a thing of beauty and might be appreciated by the Americans.

When we bought this large plot of ground for our new church, I pictured in my mind a beautiful Japanese garden in the church yard. It was a thrilling thought.

Fortunately one of my church members, Mr. Ryotaro Nishikawa, was a well-known landscape gardener in the Northwest. I went to him and explained my idea. He was enthusiastic about the garden and promised that he would contribute his services to the church.

He came to the churchyard the next day and studied the land from every angle. A few days later he was ready to show the committee a little model of the garden and explain it. It looked wonderful. They appreciated his effort and asked him to go ahead with his plans.

The first work on our garden was a stone wall in front of the chapel. A castle in Japan is surrounded by a stone wall. Mr. Nishikawa wanted the castle of God to have a stone wall. A Japanese stone wall is an architectural art, which only a man with knowledge and experience can build properly.

Mr. Tsunazo Edamatsu, one of our older church members, was an expert in this field when he was young. He became a farmer in America, but he had been a stone mason before coming here. He also offered his services. When he came to the churchyard to start the work, he was surprised and pleased that we had so many stones lying around. He checked many stones and marked all the ones he wanted to use. Volunteers carried all those marked stones to the proper places. During rain or shine this seventy-four-year-old man worked every day and completed the wall a few days before he had to leave Spokane for Japan. He was very happy when it was finished. I visited him in his house to express my appreciation.

"Reverend Shimada," he said, "I am grateful that my ability has been useful for the house of God. It is my honor and privilege to be of use to the church. I feel as if I have laid up some treasures in heaven." This old gentleman passed away in 1962, but the stone wall remains as his tribute to God.

At both ends of the stone wall Mr. Nishikawa planned beautiful rock gardens. He discovered many good rocks in our churchyard, but many of them were very heavy. Wheelbarrows were not sufficient for those that weighed 1,000 pounds or more. A few of our church members who were farmers gave their services in moving the larger rocks with their tractors.

Placing each rock exactly right on the sharp slope was very difficult. Only a professional landscaper has the necessary knowledge. Not only the position but the direction each rock is facing is important. Mr. Nishikawa taught us that each rock has a face. Some face straight forward, some look up, some look down, some have a nice profile. Rocks also have personalities. Some rocks are shy, some are haughty, some are independent, and some are dependent on others. Some are good in the center of the garden; some are suitable at the edge.

Thus, each rock should be placed in the right position and in the right direction for its character and appearance; otherwise the rocks would seem dead and the rock garden would be out of order. We learned from hard experience that a proper Japanese rock garden is not easy to make.

Besides the assistance of other volunteers, Mr. Nishikawa had two faithful issei members, Mr. Tadaichi Hayashi and Mr. Tsuneta Hayashi, who worked hard with him every day from morning to sundown all that cold, snowy winter. The rock garden was finished before spring, and even he was satisfied with it. He not only put his ability and skill in the garden but his heart as well.

"Artists paint pictures on canvas," he once said to me, "but I draw a picture on land." He was indeed an artist.

Whenever he placed a wild rock in a suitable position, the rock became alive and seemed to be speaking to us. All the rocks in the garden were once wild and worthless, but now they came to have an important part in beautifying the house of God.

Once people laughed at us because we bought worthless rocky land, but this ugly piece of land came to life through the devotion and love of our church members.

All the shrubs and trees, large and small, were gifts from our church members and friends. As we had no funds for landscaping, we could not buy anything. The church members began to uproot the plants in their own yards and transplant them around the church. The donations for the garden began to come in.

A tremendous amount of volunteer labor also went into the church building and the new parsonage, which we built on the same ground. The English-speaking division—men, women, and youths—and the older Japanese-speaking division—both men and women—united their efforts and hearts in fulfilling our dream. I especially remember the expression of friendship of Mr. Fred King, a friend of the church, who donated his skill and labor in doing the entire carpentry work in the church kitchen with the assistance of our two Mr. Hayashis, mentioned before, who were skilled in many ways.

Another beautiful story of friendship can be told of the members of Wapato Japanese Methodist Church, located about 200 miles from Spokane, where I went to preach once a month for a few years. Several of their nisei men came all the way to Spokane in the winter season when they could arrange the time to give us a helping hand in the building project. They stayed one whole week and gave their services full time.

When our building and garden were nearly completed, I received a letter from Dr. Pedersen of the Philadelphia headquarters of the Board of Mission and Church Extension of the Methodist Church. He said that he was coming to Spokane to see our new church.

I waited for the day of his coming as for the day of judgment. I remembered that I had written a strong letter to headquarters appealing for a donation of $25,000 (one-third of the original plan); so it was quite natural that they were anxious to see what the small Japanese congregation had done with the money. I imagined that the Philadelphia office had decided to send Dr. Pedersen to inspect our church. I felt nervous at the prospect.

I did not know whether he would like the Japanese landscaping in the church yard or not. He might say, "You are wasting time, energy, and money in making unnecessary things such as this strange rock garden. You should concentrate your mind on the church building only. What a fool you are." Then my whole effort and dream could be miserably shattered. Or he might say, "You are doing all right. Your church is pretty good with the garden." Then I would be richly rewarded.

Anyway, nothing would take away my love for beautifying land, which is inherent in Japanese blood.

The day before he was supposed to arrive, as I was doing some cleaning job in work clothes in my study, a gentleman came in and said, "I am Dr. Pedersen from the Philadelphia headquarters." I was shocked at his unexpected appearance a day early and did not know what to do. I was not prepared to meet him. I was in rough clothes, and my hands and face were dirty.

While I stood there speechless, Dr. Pedersen took my dirty hand with a strong grip and shook it warmly. "This is one of the most beautiful churches I have ever seen," he said. "I know how hard you have been working with your church members to make it like this. It is almost a miracle to build such a beautiful and unique church with such a small amount of money. Many congratulations, Mr. Shimada."

My heart was full of joy at his words. I am odd that way; when I am confronted with a difficulty and meet severe criticism, I can be a fighter, but when I receive a warm word, I become soft-hearted.

"Thank you very much. I am very happy to hear it from you," was all I could say at that time, but I felt a deep gratitude in my heart.

Assuring me that he would come back to our church the next day to take pictures and spend more time with me, Dr. Pedersen left.

The next day he came to our church again. This time I was all dressed up. Even though it did not make much difference in my appearance, I at least felt clean. I told him that all the church members became one in faith and in heart in building this house of God; they had done their best.

"Yes, I can see it," he said. "I tell you, this church will be the pride of our Methodist Church in America."

I thought he was just flattering me, but when I saw the November issue of *Together* (the Methodist family magazine of that time) in 1959, I realized that he really meant it. It was the 175th anniversary issue of the Methodist Church, and our church was introduced like this: "Spokane: Japanese Methodists poured love and toil into Highland Park Church, transformed craggy hillside into picturesque beauty spot to delight visitors."

I believe it was Dr. Pedersen who introduced our church to *Together* magazine. All our church members were very happy when they saw and read it.

In the April, 1959, issue of *Together*, eight pictures of our church appeared. There was a wonderful title at the top of the pictures: "With imagination and elbow grease, this congregation transformed a rocky wasteland into a bit of old Japan in Spokane."

The notes with the pictures said that the 280-member church had bought "1¹/₂ hilly acres marred by outcropping volcanic rocks . . . for the cut-rate price of $2865. . . . And into it they plowed their toil, their ingenuity, their dreams. . . . The transformation from rocks to rock gardens took fourteen months—and plenty of hard work. Members donated over 16,000 hours of labor—plus flowers, shrubs, and trees from their own yards—to grade and landscape the grounds and finish the buildings."

We held the ground-breaking service on Easter of 1957 and held our first service in the new church on Easter of 1958. We had almost completed the church building, the fellowship hall, Sunday school classrooms, the parsonage, and the gardens within a year. We were so absorbed in building our church that the year passed like a month, and when we came to ourselves and took a breath, it was another Easter.

Who could have imagined a year before that such an inspiring church would rise on the rough, rocky land? As we proceeded with the service on that Easter morning in the new sanctuary, we were strengthened in the belief that Jesus Christ was living and working through us. It was the most significant Easter service I ever had. We believed that without the help of Jesus Christ we could not have built this church.

Our fellowship hall was named Ellis Hall, and the sanctuary was named Butler Chapel, in honor of Mrs. John D. Ellis and Mrs. Alfred D. Butler, two wonderful Methodist women who had given so generously and unselfishly of themselves for the Christian nurture of our people in Spokane since the early days of our church.

One day our landscaper told me that there was still something missing from the garden. "I would like to have a nine-foot hexagon structure in the oriental style on this particular spot," he said. "It will make the balance of the garden perfect and will be the best place for a view of the garden and the church building."

While I was listening to him, a new idea came to my mind: this would be the "House of Prayer." Our new church building does not have a church tower because the type of architecture makes a tower inappropriate. To me the church tower is the symbol of prayer. Why not build the church tower here on the ground and call it the House of Prayer? People could actually pray in this hexagonal house.

Several church members donated for this small project, and the House of Prayer was made possible. To me this six-sided house really was the house of prayer. I prayed there before I went to my office in the morning, and I would go there and have a quiet time of prayer whenever my heart became heavy.

A Caucasian lady went there often and spent a quiet meditation period. "Whenever I come here from downtown," she once said to me, "I feel as if I come to an oasis in the desert. This is so quiet and peaceful; I like to come here whenever my body and mind get tired."

Such was the church in Spokane. We were proud of it, and we realized that it could never have been completed by our mortal efforts alone.

26
The Treacherous Son Returns

And then it was 1959, the year of the celebration of the 100th anniversary of Protestantism in Japan. I had to make up my mind. All of the old doubts were still with me.

I received a letter from the Reverend Mr. Kimura, saying: "Come to Japan and help the special evangelistic campaign related to the centennial." My heart was strongly moved by this letter. There was also my promise to my father.

"I must go," I said to myself. "I cannot hide forever. I will meet all the ministers and church leaders and confess my cowardice openly before them all. I will ask for forgiveness. And I will do my best to help in this historic campaign."

Putting all hesitation behind me, I went to Japan in the fall of 1959.

My brother Takeo met me at Tokyo Airport. The next day he and I took the train to Kanazawa, where my father lived. During that ride we talked of many things.

Takeo told me then, for the first time, what my story of the star had meant to him during the dark period after the death of our mother. He told me of a talk he gave at a gathering for all the junior high school students who had lost their mothers or fathers, and for all the teachers who lost parents during their childhood years. They shared their experiences, strengthening and encouraging one another.

Takeo said his talk ended something like this: "For a long time in my boyhood days I believed that a particular star was my mother. Of course, I do not believe that now, but whenever

I see that star, my heart is warm, and a happy feeling comes back to me. The brother who taught me to look up to that star is a minister in a Methodist church in Spokane, Washington, in the United States of America.

"When I lost my only daughter and was in deep sorrow, my brother in America again reached out his loving hand and brought me to America to study. It was not an easy thing to study in English at forty years of age, and there were times when I was discouraged and disappointed. But when evening came and I looked up to that same star in America, I was encouraged and strengthened. America or Japan, there is no difference. The star is the same, the star of my mother, the star of strength and encouragement. I advise you all to choose a shining star in the sky as the star of your mother or father. I think such a star will give you strength and purify your heart."

We talked of my father's deserved happiness in his second marriage. Takeo confirmed my impression that this marriage continued to be a fine thing. My stepmother took good care of my father, and for this I would always be grateful to her.

I learned that one of the two young men who manhandled me into the church at my sister's request so long ago had died before the war, and the other was a minister of a large church in northwest Japan.

My other brother and sister were doing well. Ayako was married to a prosperous farmer in Hokkaido, the northern part of Japan. Masashi, who had manufactured soap before the war, now owned a fish market in Osaka.

Kanazawa is 350 miles from Tokyo, but the ten-hour trip seemed like an hour as Takeo and I talked of things we had completely forgotten until we met each other again. Before we realized, we were only twenty-five miles from home.

My father, my stepmother, four relatives, and ten Christian friends from the old days met us at the station. Seeing them all after so many years was a warm experience.

I found my old acquaintances surprisingly aged; I believe they felt the same about me. More than a quarter of a century is a long time. My father had become more feeble, and I could tell that his life journey was coming to an end. He was so happy on this occasion, however, that he acted like a child.

I stayed with my father and stepmother for two weeks. They had a two-room apartment, with several kinds of flowers in pots; he still loved flowers. A picture of my two children hung on the wall of his room. My stepmother welcomed me even more warmly than my father. She had not attended school and even then could not write her own name, but she was a good woman with a warm heart.

I discovered that she had been remembering me in a way that seemed strange to me after my years in America. She had placed my picture on a small table in the corner of the room and every day she put a lunch in front of my picture. At supper time she took the lunch and ate it herself. She called it *kagezen*. "Kage" means shadow; "zen" means meal.

Some pious people in Japan practice kage-zen in remembrance of loved ones who have died or who are far away. My stepmother was not a religious woman, but she placed a kage-zen for me as an expression of affection. I personally see no meaning in the practice, but I treasured it as a measure of her love for me.

When I showed my father a picture of my older church members—the Japanese-speaking congregation—which was taken just two weeks before I left Spokane, he called each one by name. I was surprised at his memory after the seven years that had passed since his short visit. He himself had three large picture albums of his trip to America. Under each picture he had written a note, many with humorous comments. My father was young in spirit.

I visited the shrine that had been the scene of my first contact with false gods as a boy of six. It could hardly be called a shrine now. It had been moved about half a block from the original site and was in a bleak and gloomy little cave. There was only one idol, which was not one of the original four. I am sure I would have remembered them; that lone image was a stranger to me. I dropped a few coins in the offertory box for old times' sake. Had the original images been there still, I might have been more generous.

I made a surprising discovery about the Japanese food that I had been recalling with such longing for years; I didn't like it very well anymore.

My father knew my favorite foods, so my stepmother prepared many of the dishes I had liked so well in the past. They looked wonderful, but when I started to eat, the taste was not what I expected. At first I thought my stepmother was not a good cook, but there I did her an injustice. My father and all my relatives enjoyed the food and considered her an excellent cook.

An old friend held a welcome party for me in the best restaurant in town. I had always remembered it for its delicious food. Now I did not enjoy the banquet.

My brother Masashi owned a fish market and remembering how fond I was of all kinds of fish, he brought the best for us. One was *tai*—considered the best by Japanese—and tuna, and other types not known in America. They were cooked in the traditional way for my enjoyment, but the taste did not equal my anticipation.

I decided that I was really getting old.

Oddly, the Japanese food I enjoyed most had not been served during my childhood. I liked *nigiri-zushi*, a dish of small rice balls seasoned with vinegar mix and topped with different kinds of raw fish, which was popular in Tokyo. I also liked noodles in soup, topped with fried prawns.

On August 23, 1959, a special meeting was held for me in my native church. When I entered the building with my father, I felt that I must have come to the wrong place. I had always considered it large and beautiful; now the same church seemed small and dingy.

Before the meeting started I wandered through every room. One had been my Sunday school classroom. There I remembered a boy whom I had taught. He had gone on to become a minister, following my example, I believe. He also had been cast out of his home because of his faith. I learned that he had been killed during the war.

This visit to the native church where I was born spiritually and had tried to teach the boys and girls the joy of Christianity was an inspiration which renewed my strength.

My father was asked to preside over the service that evening; the minister assisted him because of his age. My father made a speech when he introduced me to the congregation. He said much the same things that he had said in his radio address in Spokane, describing his early enmity to Christianity and his conversion through the discovery of the virtue of Christian practices in America.

He finished by saying, "In the past when I was asked what my son was doing in America, I was ashamed to say that he was a Christian minister; I told people instead that he was teaching the Japanese language there. After my visit to America and my conversion, my shame changed to a great pride. Since then I have said to them, 'My son is a minister; he is doing God's work in America.' And this evening, with the same pride and joy, I present the Reverend Mr. Shimada, my son, your guest speaker from America."

I listened to those beautiful words of introduction as to a great poem. My heart was full of joy and gratitude to God. I felt that my father's words and feelings made the trip from America to Japan worthwhile. I felt, in the spiritual sense, almost like General MacArthur. Spiritually, I too "had returned."

That evening, in the presence of the congregation and that wonderful father who, though so old in years he could scarcely walk, was so young in spirit that he looked on me as his spiritual father, I gave my testimony.

After receiving a blessing from my father, I started my work for the evangelistic campaign. I felt that I was ready to face such criticism as I might receive from my brother ministers for my earlier decision to remain in America.

During the months of September and October, I visited seventy churches and five mission schools in Japan. I had only two days off during this period, but it was a deeply rewarding experience.

In Hiroshima I found amazingly little bitterness over the atomic bomb. It was there, of course, but it was fading away. The city maintains a large museum in Peace Park, with pictures and materials that show the damage that was done. The purpose of this exhibit is not to remind people of the past horror of the bomb but to show the world the terrible danger of atomic war.

It is the hope of the Hiroshima people that no other city will share this experience again. Sincere people in Hiroshima and all over Japan are hoping and trying to produce a spirit of peace from the disaster of the atomic bomb. The communists have attempted to use the story of the bomb for their anti-American propaganda. They did not touch on the treachery of Pearl Harbor but told only the Hiroshima story. They were not successful in leading the people of Japan to hate America.

By the summer of 1945, the whole world knew that Japan was out of food, out of ammunition, out of just about everything necessary for survival and that the nation would not last much longer. While it is known that one of the scientists involved in the development of the atomic bomb vehemently objected to the use of it on humans, it was dropped on Hiroshima, where women, children, the aged, and the sick made up the bulk of this densely populated city as most of the able-bodied men had been sent to the battlefields. Two days later another bomb was dropped on the city of Nagasaki. What a great sacrifice for the victims of atomic bombs in Hiroshima and in Nagasaki if a nuclear war could be averted because the disastrous outcome has been witnessed by the world! The world now understands what a single nuclear weapon, powerful enough to destroy a thousand Hiroshimas, can do.

With the passage of the McCarran-Walter Act in 1952, Asians in America were given the right to become naturalized citizens. It was reported that over 90 percent of the Japanese in America became naturalized. I myself gained the American citizenship in the year 1954, hoping to become a good citizen. I was proud of my citizenship. America was really a great nation at that time. In fact, America was the greatest nation in human history. America was the richest nation in the world economically. America was helping the suffering nations in Europe financially and materially. The civilization of America was superior to that of any nation in the world. American Christians were sending many missionaries to many places in the world. To me America was an ideal nation, and I became a citizen of this great and wonderful nation. Naturally my heart was full of gratitude.

However, I could not ignore the fact that America dropped an atomic bomb on humans—a sin that surely cannot escape some form of punishment from God. As an American citizen I was enjoying the privileges and benefits of living in this wonderful land, but was I willing to take any part of the responsibility for this sinful act? As I wrestled with this problem, a strong feeling came to me that as a true American citizen I must accept the punishment as well as the privileges. When I came to this realization, strange to say, I began to love America wholeheartedly.

From Hiroshima I went to Chinzei Gakuin High School in Hayasame near Nagasaki in Kyushu, where I was invited to speak. Mr. Samejima, the principal of the school, decided to take advantage of my visit and hold a two-day religious emphasis campaign in the school.

As an expression of appreciation for my services, Mr. Samejima took me to Unzen National Park the next day. He showed me a spot where a rugged old cross stood on a rock. Three hundred years ago many Christians (Catholics) were thrown from that rock into the extremely hot water at the bottom. Today no one knows how many Christians were killed there. Some say several hundred; others say several thousand.

"Japan has the most Christian martyrs in history," Mr. Samejima said. "If the ancient Roman Empire became a Christian nation through the blood of the Christian martyrs, then Japan should also become a Christian nation, because Japan has more martyrs than the Roman Empire."

Today there is no hot water at the bottom of the rock, but the rugged cross still remains on the same spot. It is an inspiration to me even today.

While I was in Tokyo I had a rare opportunity to see the Imperial Garden from corner to corner. The Vice Grand Chamberlain, a Christian, arranged this special visit for me and sent one of his assistants to guide me. The guide took me everywhere and explained everything to me.

There was a large vegetable garden. "In America many rich people have gardens like this," I said, "because they prefer really fresh vegetables to those from the store. I suppose the Emperor and Empress felt the same way."

"No, that isn't it," the guide said. "Of course, they eat them too, but that isn't their main concern. You see, the workers in the Imperial Palace have very small salaries. The Emperor and Empress know this, but they cannot do anything about it because they themselves do not have enough money now. Before the war when the Imperial Family was one of the richest families in the world, our salaries were good. Now the Emperor cannot raise our salaries, but he wants to help us, so he had these vegetables planted in his garden. They are for us, his workers.

"Actually, it does not help us a great deal financially, but we really appreciate the Emperor's concern and kind thoughts. After the war many employees left the Imperial house because of the small salaries, but I stay because I love and respect the Emperor. I personally think he is the kindest person in the whole world."

As he finished this beautiful story I saw about thirty women in white aprons walking together. I asked my guide if they were special visitors to the garden.

"No," he said, "they are volunteer workers in the Imperial house. They come from all over Japan: from Hokkaido in the uppermost north and from Kyushu far to the south. They pay their own train fare and hotel expenses. They are permitted to serve for only a few days because women are already scheduled six months in advance for the privilege of giving this service. They are not paid a cent, but many are very anxious to serve."

His explanation made the women in white aprons look something like angels to me.

While the Reverend Taro Goto (my friend from the Topaz center, also working on the campaign) and I were in Tokyo, the former Methodist ministers and workers held an official reception for us on the Aoyama Gakuin University campus. Bishop Abe, the chairman, welcomed us warmly as did the fifty ministers who attended.

In reply the Reverend Mr. Goto said to them, "The United States of America and Japan are sister nations today, and some cities in America and in Japan have become sister cities. If some of our churches and some of yours became sister churches and helped each other, it would be most significant. If all the churches in Japan had sister churches in America, it would bring a blessing not only to the churches but to both nations."

And then it was time for me to speak. I had been welcomed all over Japan in the most friendly fashion, with no one showing the slightest inclination to criticize me for my decision to remain in America. I had not yet, however, discussed the matter openly.

"I have been given an opportunity to visit Japan twice before this," I began, and went on to tell them the story of my doubts and fears. I finished "In spite of my sense of unworthiness, you ministers have not blamed or criticized me. You have welcomed me as though I were a young brother returning from a vacation. Your warm attitude makes my heart even heavier. I know that you have endured much suffering and made many sacrifices. The thought of them makes me ashamed. Please forgive me for not returning to share your suffering."

There was a long silence in the room when I finished. I saw tears being wiped away.

After the reception several ministers told me that my talk had made them humble. They too had felt shame over their conduct. They felt that they had not done the work for their ministry as bravely as they should because of the pressure of the militarists. Humility brought us together in union.

I especially remember the comments of one elderly minister. "Your testimony and experience are utterly unique," he said. "There were many Japanese Christians who were cast out from their homes, so this point does not make your case unique. Neither does the conversion and baptism of your father; other Christians have done this. You are, however, the only minister who invited his father to America, converted him to Christianity there, baptized him, and sent him back to Japan. Your accomplishment took twenty-five years of prayer and patience, but it was worthwhile. The stage was widened from Japan to America, covering the Pacific Ocean. This whole stage was necessary for the wonderful drama of fulfilling your promise to God. In this your experience is utterly unique in the history of Christianity in Japan."

I myself feel that my visit to Japan was a success and a blessing to me. It brought great joy to my father. My confession before the ministers warmed their hearts and mine, brought us closer together, and dissolved all barriers that possibly may have existed.

Perhaps most important of all, I feel that the testimony of my father's conversion was a constructive contribution to Christianity in Japan.

27

The Death of My Father

I spent my last few days in Japan with my father. He had been praying for me while I was traveling for the evangelistic mission. When I came back to him, he looked much weaker to me. I took him to the doctor. The doctor said that nothing was wrong; he was simply getting old and weak. I knew he was dying. I tried my best to comfort him and encourage him. He himself knew that his life was coming to an end.

The day before I left him he said, "I am the happiest man in the whole world. I am grateful to God, and I am thankful to you for everything you have done for me. You are a good son. I hope you are a faithful servant of God until death. I know that the end of my life is approaching. I feel it. You may receive the news of my death in America someday soon, but please do not be sorrowful because I am not at all afraid of death. I am rather waiting for the day to meet my Savior in heaven."

He had learned the Christian lesson that death is simply a gateway to heaven. That evening I bought the choicest meat and cooked sukiyaki for him, hoping he would enjoy it. He ate only a little and said, "I ate a lot. It was certainly a delicious sukiyaki."

The next day I said "sayonara" to him in Japanese, and he replied "good-bye" in English. He knew two words of English: good-bye and thank-you.

I looked at him. He smiled at me and said, "I will see you in heaven."

I knew he really meant it.

"Father," I said, "I will come back to you in three years. Promise me to make every effort to live three more years."

He smiled again. "All right, I will promise to do my best."

And thus we were separated from each other. I returned to America on November 19, 1959. He passed away on Palm Sunday of the following year. When the telegram came to us from Japan, I was in the church office preparing for the services. My wife knew immediately that my father had passed away. She kept the telegram in her pocket until all the Palm Sunday services were over. I had three special services on that day: one in the morning, one in the afternoon, and one in the evening. I was quite tired when I returned to the parsonage after the last service.

"Are you all through with your services?" my wife asked.

"Yes, I am all through now."

"I have bad news," she said. "Here it is."

She gave me the telegram; Father had passed away. I had known it would be soon; yet when the news actually came, I could not at first control my sorrow. I trembled with emotion.

"I got the telegram this morning right after you left home," my wife said. "I knew your responsibilities were heavy today. I kept it until now so that you would not be disturbed while conducting the services. I hope you are not angry with me."

"Thank you for your consideration. I am glad you kept it until now."

I strolled alone in the church garden, renewing my appreciation of my father and communing with his spirit.

According to my stepmother's letter, which came later, my father was cheerful on that last day. After a light supper, as he stood up to go to the washroom, his heart stopped, and he died. He was seventy-nine years old. The doctor said that his was the perfectly natural death for an old man.

His ashes were placed in our new family tomb in Osaka, erected by my two brothers and myself while I was visiting there in 1959. On the tombstone we placed this verse from the Book of Job in the Old Testament: "The Lord has given and the Lord has taken away. Blessed be the name of the Lord."

Yes, God gave me the best father in the world, and God in his wisdom took him away from me to the heavenly kingdom.

28

To Pay the Debt of Love

The year 1971 was a significant year for me and my wife. On New Year's Day we made a decision to retire at the annual conference, which would be held in June at the University of Puget Sound in Tacoma, Washington, and go to Japan as self-supporting missionaries. We were sure that the pension from the United Methodist Church and the social security benefits would be just about enough to support our living in Japan. So we would not receive any salary or compensation for our services there.

I had a huge debt of love in Japan. I had to pay it back before it was too late. When I came to America for my further study, my church members, friends, and even professors of my alma mater gave me money as farewell gifts. The monetary gifts totaled $300, not much even at that time, but their love to me was so great that I could not adequately express my deep gratitude in words. They certainly expected me to come back to Japan when I finished my study, and I also wanted to return to Japan. I had no desire to stay in America at that time. I certainly had no idea that the war would break out between Japan and America while I was studying. But the unexpected war changed everything. As I explained earlier in my story, after the war I decided to stay and work with the Japanese people in America.

I became more and more interested and involved in the ministry to Japanese-Americans, and before I realized it, I had stayed twenty-five years in America after the war. However, all this time a still, small voice was whispering in my heart day and night: "You are a traitor to your friends in Japan. All the Japanese ministers suffered under miserable living conditions in the postwar era for Christ and his kingdom, but you have been living comfortably in America. Aren't you ashamed of yourself?" The voice was small but strong enough to hurt my conscience. So at the beginning of 1971, we decided to retire and go back to Japan.

When I wrote to Bishop Maynard Sparks, our area bishop, about my decision, he aksed if I would not consider going as a missionary from the Board of Missions of the United Methodist Church. I was deeply moved by his kind consideration, but I wanted to make my own plans and serve accordingly as I knew the situation in Japan. The bishop understood me and let me retire. I would be retiring at sixty-five years of age.

There was a Christian Women's College in Nishinomiya, the sister city of Spokane. It was this school, Seiwa Women's College (now a coeducational school called Seiwa College) that I wished to serve.

The city of Nishinomiya is located midway between Osaka and Kobe. I had done the initial liaison work that led to the affiliation of Nishinomiya and Spokane as sister cities. On April 15, 1962, the Spokane-Nishinomiya City Affiliation Ceremony was held in Nishinomiya, at which occasion I was given the honor of delivering a congratulatory address along with such dignitaries as the Foreign Minister of the Japanese government, the American Consul General of Kobe-Osaka, and the Governor of Hyogo Prefecture, to which prefecture Nishinomiya belongs.

The president of Seiwa, Dr. Michiko Yamakawa, the most dedicated Christian woman I have ever known, had been a good friend of mine in Christ. Therefore I wrote to her explaining our desires and hopes. She understood us and replied that she would welcome us.

At the beginning of September, 1971, we were in Japan. This was my sixth visit to Japan. Since 1959, my faithful ethnic Japanese church in Spokane, the Highland Park United Methodist Church, had enabled me to make five preaching missions to Japan. Each time it was for a period of two months (the years I made such trips I voluntarily did not take my one-month vacation). One of these trips was in connection with the world tour including a visit to the Holy Land.

On September 4, we met President Yamakawa at our future living quarters on the Seiwa Women's College campus. We exchanged our greetings warmly. Our house was a combination of American and Japanese style. It looked like a comfortable home for us.

The president gave me the schedule. My main course was "The Life and Teachings of Jesus Christ" for the second-year class. There was no suitable textbook on this subject in the Japanese language, because Japan is not a Christian nation; so I had to give a lecture each time. Another responsibility was to teach English (translating English into Japanese) to the third-year class. I also was asked to teach homiletics to the third-year students in the theological department. I had studied homiletics in the seminaries—one year in Kwansei Gakuin University, one year in Southern Methodist University, one year in Boston University, and one year in Pacific School of Religion. I thought I was qualified to teach that course.

The president asked my wife to teach piano since they needed another piano teacher in the preschool education department. Seiwa is the school to produce kindergarten teachers, and piano is a required course. Nobuko had taught piano before our marriage, so she gladly accepted the task. She also was asked to teach English conversation to several classes of elementary age students who had graduated from the kindergartens affiliated with Seiwa Women's College. They came to these kindergartens (there were two of them) after school for the English conversation classes.

All the teachers and professors at Seiwa were Christian, and we were made to feel at home. However, most of the students were not Christians. They had come to Seiwa because it was among the schools highly recommended by the education department of the Japanese government for those who wished to become kindergarten teachers. Since it was a Christian college "The Life and Teachings of Jesus Christ" was a required course. Naturally many of the students were not interested in this course. Some bravely fell asleep in the class. Personally I was rather broad-minded about these sleeping students because I myself often fell asleep during the faculty meetings.

One day I told the class, "I do not mind seeing some of you sleeping peacefully and innocently, but please don't snore while sleeping. It is not an attractive sight for beautiful girls like you to snore."

They all laughed, and strange to say, after that they stopped sleeping. I also realized that I had better change my style of lecturing because most of them did not have a Christian background.

The English class was easy to teach. However, the book they were using as the textbook was *Baby and Child Care* by Dr. Benjamin Spock, chosen by my predecessor, a woman professor. I often found myself in uncomfortable situations, translating some of the passages in the book, and I found some students giggling shyly behind their books. The next semester I changed the teaching materials to a book of short stories and a book of essays, and the teacher and students enjoyed them together thoroughly.

Typical of a Christian college, chapel hour was held daily, and I was often given the opportunity to preach during the worship services for the students and faculty. Besides my work at Seiwa Women's College, on many weekends I went to the churches in different parts of Japan to preach. My church in Spokane had given us $3,000 ($1,000 each from the English-speaking division, Japanese-speaking division, and Women's Society) as farewell gifts. We used $1,000 for our plane fares, and we took the remaining $2,000 to Japan as my evangelistic fund. This fund supported my preaching trips, paying for my traveling fares and lodging that I did not wish to impose on the host churches. I did not accept any honorariums as this was to be my service to the churches in Japan. I believe I was able to visit about forty churches on these preaching trips, covering the northern part of Kyushu, the central part of Shikoku, Hiroshima-Okayama area, Kobe-Osaka area, Nagoya area, and Tokyo.

Dr. E. Stanley Jones, a great American Christian leader, made his tenth and last visit to Japan in November, 1971, at the age of eighty-eight. We had been at Seiwa Women's College only two months when he visited Seiwa on November 8 as a guest speaker. We remembered how he had come to Topaz Relocation Center in Utah during the war to encourage us Japanese-American internees. He did not have the vitality he had then, but he was still full of enthusiasm and compassion.

My wife and I went to see him after the chapel hour. Nobuko said, "Dr. Jones, we had the privilege of hearing you speak in Topaz Relocation Center during the war."

Immediately tears welled in Dr. Jones' eyes. "Do you remember what I said?" he asked Nobuko.

"Yes. You spoke about the strength and courage of an eagle— how it soars higher and higher, flying against the storm."

We were again touched by the warmth of this great man's character.

I said to him, "Dr. Jones, you said that someday Japanese-Americans will become popular in America, and you were right. What you said has become a reality." I said this to him with confidence, for the story of the conscientious and loyal Japanese-Americans after the war is truly a success story.

Dr. Jones seemed pleased and smiled.

President Yamakawa invited us to have lunch with her and Dr. Jones. It was a simple lunch of soup and sandwiches in her office, which the aged Dr. Jones enjoyed very much. He had suffered a light stroke in recent years, we were told, and cared for only light food.

I recalled that in the prewar period when Dr. Jones was serving the people in India as an American missionary, he had an understanding for the problems of Japan. He had the idea that then sparsely populated New Guinea should be leased to Japan for ninety-nine years. Then the overpopulated nation could send her people there and develop the new land. Of course, Australia might not have approved of the idea.

After lunch Dr. Yamakawa asked Nobuko to accompany Dr. Jones to the Oriental Hotel in Kobe, where he was staying. I had to teach a class after the lunch period, so I could not go, but Professor Matsunaga, head of the religion department, would drive his car. Nobuko had admired Dr. E. Stanley Jones as a great Christian figure since her youth, and it was hard to believe that she was sitting side by side with him in a car and talking with him. Dr. Jones died a few years later. We cherish the memories of that meeting with him in Japan.

Christmas season was the most joyous time for us. Since we lived on the campus of a Christian college, it might have been natural, but it seemed almost strange to be saturated in Christmas spirit in this non-Christian nation. There were pageants, Christmas services, Christmas concerts, Christmas programs in the Seiwa-affiliated kindergartens. All were presented in Japanese, of course. There were also dormitory Christmas parties. A group of carolers came to our house one night from the junior college dormitory and another night from the four-year college dorm. There were forty voices in each group of young women students. Each one carried a lighted candle, and they sang several carols. They sang beautifully in Japanese. It was the first time for Nobuko to hear Christmas carolers sing in Japanese. We received a notice that the dormitory carolers would sing in front of our house; so Nobuko decorated the tree in the front yard with colored flickering Christmas lights, and she baked hundreds of American cookies to give to these lovely carolers. In Osaka and Kobe there were presentations of Handel's *Messiah*. Christmas in the Christian schools and churches brought its full meaning to the people, but downtown Christmas was a time of merriment and good business. "Jingle Bells" and "Santa Claus Is Coming to Town" could be heard in department stores—all in Japanese translation—but Christmas carols were rarely heard.

In the first Christmas season in Japan, Nobuko went to buy a Christmas tree. They were being sold in flower shops. She noticed that all the trees had roots, ready to be planted. She wanted a tree without the roots like in America, which would decorate the living room during the Christmas season and then be thrown away.

"Do you have a Christmas tree without the roots?" asked my wife.

"Without the roots!" the woman florist exclaimed in astonishment. Then, referring to the tree as if it were a child she pleaded, "Please decorate this and after the Christmas season is over, please plant it somewhere in the corner of your yard, and please give it loving care."

That day Nobuko brought home a small, living Christmas tree with roots wrapped with a piece of burlap. She placed it in a pan and watered it and placed it on a table. She said that she picked that one because it had the best shape. It was the smallest tree I had ever seen, but cute, I thought. After Christmas we carefully planted it in the corner of our backyard. The needles were falling, and I said, "There is a fifty-fifty chance of this tree surviving."

"Well," my wife shrugged her shoulders, "we'll see."

She watered the little ailing tree with care and love as the florist had asked her to, and to our delight it began to grow. In our second Christmas season we dug it out and placed it on a lower table. The third Christmas we had to place it on the floor. The fourth and last Christmas in Japan, the tree had grown so tall and sturdy that it was difficult to dig out, and the tip of the tree almost touched the ceiling. Nobuko had to buy more ornaments and lights. We knew that we would not be there the following Christmas, but we planted the tree in the yard as we did before. Since our departure we have not heard about the tree, which brought us Christmas joy during our sojourn in Japan.

My teaching schedule in the final year at Seiwa Women's College became very heavy for two reasons: 1) I started to give a new series of lectures on Christianity in the newly established graduate class. 2) The dean of the theological department, Dr. Shinichi Matsunaga, went to Southern Methodist University in Dallas, Texas, for his further study, and the president asked me to take over his main course, "The Life and Thoughts of Saint Paul." These two lecture series were extra.

During the day I gave lectures, and at night I had to prepare the lectures for the next day. I became almost worn out. I lost my health. During that year I had in my care over 500 students. One morning I just could not get up. I could not move my body. I felt a severe pain around my waist. With my wife's help I finally got up and went to school to give the lectures. After school I went to my doctor who had been taking care of my hypertension. The doctor advised me to go back to America as soon as possible because Japan was not suitable to my health.

I decided to return to America after my third and last year was over. On the morning of the graduation ceremony in March, 1975 (in Japan the new school year begins in April), a group of students representing the junior college graduates approached us with 1000 *origami* cranes. They had made the tiny cranes by folding papers in varied colors. They were strung and tied in a bunch. They looked like a bunch of wisteria flowers in myriad colors.

One of them, representing the entire graduating class, said, "We appreciated your services to Seiwa Women's College. We put our love and respect and admiration into these cranes. Would you please take them with you to America? These cranes represent our hearts and our prayers for you."

My heart was bursting with joy. I accepted the 1000 cranes with deep appreciation. The crane has a special meaning in Japan. It is the symbol of longevity.

In Hiroshima Peace Park there is a monument for children who died in the atomic blast. This is the story I heard which inspired the erection of this monument: A little girl who was a victim of the atomic bomb believed that she would be cured if she made 1000 origami cranes. She started making them by folding each little crane with the colored paper, but before she could finish them she died. When the children across the nation heard this story, they began to make origami cranes and sent them to the children's monument. These cranes were the expression of their sympathy to all the children who were victims of the atomic bomb. There were tens of thousands of these colorful paper cranes by the monument when we visited the Peace Park during our sojourn in Japan. We were told that many times the old, faded cranes were replaced by the new ones as they arrived from all over Japan.

Another group of students brought two small but heavy albums and said, "We students of the four-year college collected 300 letters written to you." They were written on uniform cards and bound into two thick albums. "We would like to go to America with you," they continued, "but it is impossible. So would you please take these 300 *yosegaki* (collection of letters) with you? These are our love and prayers for you."

My heart was moved again with deep gratitude. I accepted

the two albums with tears.

The day of the graduation in March, 1975, was our last day at Seiwa Women's College. The chairman of the Board of Trustees presented to us a certificate of appreciation. He read it before the audience of students, teachers, parents, and other guests. My wife and I were profoundly impressed by the words in the certificate. When it was presented to us, I told the audience that this certificate would be treasured in the Shimada family and that it would be handed down to our son and then to our grandson. There was a big applause in the packed auditorium. As a farewell gift the school presented to me a splendid scroll with a *sumi* (black ink) painting of mountains and river and a gorgeous *kutani* vase; to my wife they presented a beautiful silk kimono and *obi* (a broad sash worn with a kimono).

There was a big crowd at the Osaka airport near Nishinomiya to bid us farewell. It was during the spring vacation, but many Seiwa Women's College students were there as well as President Yamakawa and the professors and many Nishinomiya city officials, including Mayor and Mrs. Tatsuuma. All my relatives in Osaka and some of my old Osaka church members and our friends were there also.

My wife received several beautiful bouquets and gifts, which later had to be taken in a cart to the airplane. Professor Yanagihara, head of the music department of Seiwa, led the group in the singing of the first stanza of "God Be with You Till We Meet Again." Mayor Tatsuuma then volunteered to lead them in the three thunderous *banzai* cheers, wishing us long life. Thus we left Japan, receiving many warm blessings. Our three-and-a-half years in Japan left us with rich memories. I came away with a strong conviction that I had paid back the heavy debt of love. The strong but whispering voice calling me a "traitor" disappeared from my heart forever.

We returned to America and decided to live in Seattle, Washington, simply because our daughter and son lived there. Our daughter Gloria, who felt that her decision to become a teacher of blind children was a calling, is happy in her work. She is married to a fine Japanese-American pediatric cardiologist, Dr. Isamu Kawabori, who is on the faculty of the University of Washington Medical School. Our son Justin is married to a lovely Chinese-American, Fay Dong, a school teacher. When we returned from Japan he was studying for a Ph.D. degree in Business Administration at the University of Washington, which he earned a few years later. He is presently enjoying his work in the academic field.

About a year after our return to America, President Yamakawa and Seiwa Women's College published a book titled *Professor Shimada in Seiwa Women's College and His Sermons in the Chapel*. It is a little book of 187 pages. There is a picture of my wife and me holding the 1000 cranes on the first page of the book. Then twenty of my many sermons follow, and then thirty yosegaki from the 300 letters conclude the book. I was very happy to see that my twenty sermons are embraced by 1000 cranes and thirty yosegaki.

Here I have translated three of the yosegaki for the interest of my children:

To Professor and Mrs. Shimada:
I have learned Christian love from both of you. Mrs. Shimada is my favorite lady. I want to be an affectionate lady like Mrs. Shimada, and I like to become a sweet wife like her. Whenever I saw you both together on the road or on the campus, I felt something warm in my heart. I learned how to play the piano from you, Mrs. Shimada. You played the piano not only with your fingers but with your heart also. I will try to play with my heart too.

To Professor Shimada:
I have learned a great deal from your lectures on Saint Paul. I have been interested in the life of Saint Paul ever since I became a Christian. When I was listening to your lectures, I felt as if I were actually seeing Saint Paul in your life and character. I realized that in your last year at Seiwa you put more power and more spirit in your lectures and in your sermons, and I was deeply inspired in the class as well as in the chapel. I became a Christian two years ago; so I am still a baby Christian, but I will try hard to become a sincere Christian like Professor Shimada.

To Professor Shimada:
I was always inspired and encouraged by your sermons in the chapel. One particular sermon really enlightened my heart. You said in it that there are large stones and small stones in any stone wall of any Japanese castle. People may think that large stones are more important than the small ones, but that is wrong. A

small stone is equally important as a large stone. When I heard that sermon, I felt as if a new bright world appeared before me. I made up my mind to live bravely without fear, because God loves even me, this small stone. It is indeed a blessing to me that I entered the Seiwa Women's College and came to know you.

I am humbled by these letters. They have overestimated me beyond any word.

29

The Fifth Order of the Sacred Treasure

When we settled in Seattle, Consul General Uchida was in command of the Japanese Consulate in Seattle. Mrs. Uchida was a former graduate of Seiwa Women's College. So when the school published my book, President Yamakawa sent a copy to her.

Several months later Mr. Uchida received a new appointment from the Japanese government as the ambassador to Senegal in Africa. It was several days before their departure that we received an invitation to dinner in the official residence of the consulate general. We accepted the invitation of now Ambassador and Mrs. Uchida with deep appreciation.

When we arrived at the official residence, Mr. and Mrs. Uchida welcomed us cordially and led us to the beautiful reception room, where I saw the pictures of the Emperor and Empress of Japan on the wall. I stood before the pictures and spontaneously bowed deeply. I was not worshiping the Emperor. I simply expressed my deep respect to him in that way.

I believe that Emperor Hirohito is the most sincere person in Japan. All through his life I understand that he abstained from drinking and smoking. He was faithful only to the Empress, keeping the principle of monogamy. His grandfather, Emperor Meiji, had kept several concubines in his palace, but Emperor Hirohito never indulged in immoral behavior. He is a perfect gentleman, and I feel a pride in him as the Emperor of my native land.

Emperor Hirohito is a peace-loving emperor. Before the war there was a special meeting in the presence of the Emperor in Japan. He did not call that meeting. The cabinet members, military leaders, and other dignitaries in various fields of the Japanese government forced him to hold that meeting to discuss whether they should start a war against the United States or not. The Emperor clearly expressed his idea against the war. There was no reason for those present not to understand his stance against the war.

Yet the militarists and politicians plunged the nation into war, trampling the Emperor's wish and making his existence equal to a robot. To them the Emperor was a living puppet. They completely sealed his mouth during the war.

When the atomic bombs finally brought Japan to surrender, some of the military leaders should have stood before the microphone to announce the surrender, but not one of the militarists would take that miserable job. They knew that all the Japanese people would get angry at the army and a riot would start all over Japan. Once a riot started, no one would be able to control the mad mob. So the militarists placed that final responsibility on the Emperor. When they started the war, they disregarded the Emperor's wish, but when the war came to an end with a miserable defeat, they made the Emperor the final responsible person and left the most miserable task to him.

The Emperor did not blame any of the militarists. He took the whole responsibility upon his shoulders and announced the unconditional surrender of Japan to the people. Some ultra-militarists started a riot, but the people did not follow them because the surrender was announced by the Emperor, and they knew that it was the will of the Emperor. Because of the influence of Emperor Hirohito, Japan became a quiet nation in one day. Thus General MacArthur was able to enter the land of Japan without any trouble.

Some nations in the world wanted to arrest Emperor Hirohito as the number-one war criminal and put him on trial in the International War Criminal Court. Russia, England, France, Canada and some other nations liked the idea and started to put heavy pressure upon General MacArthur to do so. President Truman's attitude toward this matter was ambivalent.

Around that time Emperor Hirohito visited General MacArthur at his headquarters in Tokyo. Naturally many people in the world thought that the Emperor came to General MacArthur to appeal for his life. But the Emperor said to General MacArthur, "I am the one who should take the whole responsibility. Please punish me severely and save the lives of my people."

When General MacArthur heard these words of the Emperor, he was moved and later said that he was so impressed that the very bones within him were shaking and that he realized that Emperor Hirohito was a gentleman on the highest rank in Japan. I read about this story in several articles.

General MacArthur was so deeply inspired by Emperor Hirohito that soon after that confrontation he sent a wire to President Truman, saying that he "will not arrest the Emperor. The Emperor is the one who can save Japan, not I." President Truman accepted his idea reluctantly.

I myself respect the Emperor sincerely and profoundly. In the history of Japan there has been no such emperor as Hirohito among the 122 emperors before him. So with deep admiration and respect I stood before the picture of Emperor Hirohito in the consulate general's residence and bowed deeply. It was not an artificial bow to be seen by Mr. and Mrs. Uchida. It was a natural response to my profound respect for him.

We were led to the beautiful dining room, where we enjoyed an authentic Japanese dinner of many courses. I do not quite remember all the dishes that were served. I only recall that the dinner was delicious, but my wife remembers most of it, she says. According to her there was the clear soup, served in a beautiful, black, lacquered bowl with a gold design on the cover. Then came the *chawanmushi*, a custard-like dish made of chicken stock and egg with chicken meat, shrimp, and some vegetables steamed in a beautiful, covered, porcelain bowl. There was the dish of *sashimi*, a prepared raw tuna fish with garnishes. Nobuko says that what impressed her about the vegetable dish was the carrot, artistically cut out in the form of a plum blossom. Japanese have a way of preparing the food with artistry, serving each dish in separate china. A trout was served in a lovely rectangular plate, and Mr. and Mrs. Uchida ate the fish so neatly with the lacquered chopsticks that only the head and the bone remained on the dish like an etching. Nobuko recalls that she was rather embarrassed by the clumsy manner in which we ate the fish. There were other dishes which she cannot remember exactly, but finally came the *teri-yaki* beef, a bowl of rice, and a cup of deluxe green tea. Everything was served in an authentic Japanese dish.

After the dinner we moved to the room overlooking the Puget Sound. It was a beautiful view with the Space Needle, Seattle's landmark, on the left side. Mr. Uchida asked many things about me and my work. I did not know why he was interested in my life so much at that time. Mrs. Uchida and my wife enjoyed talking about Seiwa Women's College and about some of her old teachers who were still there. After a wonderful and memorable evening we returned home. Soon after that Mr. and Mrs. Uchida returned to Japan and then went to Senegal, Africa, as the Ambassador of Japan.

A few weeks later I received a letter from one of the Japanese consuls in Seattle, asking me to see him. I went to the consulate office, not knowing why he wanted to see me.

He said to me, "Ambassador Uchida asked me to recommend you to the Japanese government to receive the decoration from the Emperor for your work and services, and he left with me the materials." He then asked me personal questions about when and where I was born, when I came to America, what schools I graduated from, about my marriage and children, and so forth.

Now I realized clearly why Mr. Uchida had asked me many questions when we were invited to dinner, and I deeply appreciated his kind consideration. A few months later I was officially informed that I was a recipient of The Fifth Order of the Sacred Treasure decoration from the Emperor. I was extremely happy when I was so informed. The official ceremony for the delivery of the certificate of decoration and the medal was held in the official residence of the consul general. I took my wife and daughter Gloria with me to the ceremony. The new consul general officiated at the ceremony. There were a few other persons there to receive a similar honor.

When my name was called, I went before the consul general in a humble attitude and reverently received the certificate of decoration and the medal. I felt a profound happiness when I realized that the honor was coming from Emperor Hirohito, for whom I have high respect. It was truly a great honor and wonderful privilege to receive the decoration from him.

• • • • • •

Yes, a little stone on a road in a poor section of Kanazawa in Japan was picked up by Jesus Christ and has been used as his servant. That little stone has been crying out in the name of Jesus Christ throughout his life in the land of America as well as in Japan.

Despite his weaknesses he followed one straight road of faith. And it was his wife Nobuko who always stood beside him and supported him, even in times of crisis. He is now blessed with four grandchildren: Gloria's two daughters, Kimiko and Mariko; and Justin's daughter and son, Lia and Ken. Whenever he is surrounded by his four grandchildren, he is in heaven.

• • • • • •

> "I tell you, if these were silent,
> the very stones would cry out."
> —Luke 19:40